SUNDAY GOSPEL

doodle notebook

© Copyright 2022 Catechetical Chameleon

doodle notes®

learning benefits of visual note-taking

stronger **focus**

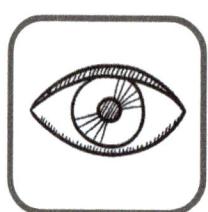
retention through dual coding

mental connections

memory **boost**

communication between **brain** hemispheres

building long-term memories

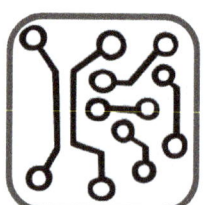
activated **neural** pathways

increased **creativity** & alertness

associative recognition

picture superiority **effect**

relaxation **benefits**

problem solving skills boost

The Gospel Doodle Note Book lets students use creativity to learn more about each Sunday Gospel and reflect on it.

As they color, doodle, and pray their way through the year's Gospels, students will explore both factual information and personal applications of the Gospel message in their own lives.

This book is perfect for a Sunday School Faith Formation class, a Catholic school, homeschool, or even just for personal use.

Terms of Use

Thanks so much for purchasing this book!

This resource is licensed to be used by a single student only.

All rights reserved.

Copying pages is prohibited.

For a PDF ebook version that you can print and copy, you can purchase a teacher license at gospeldoodlenotes.com

© Copyright 2022
Catechetical Chameleon

Clip Art & Font Credit

Sunday Gospel doodle notebook

doodle notebook

What's Included?

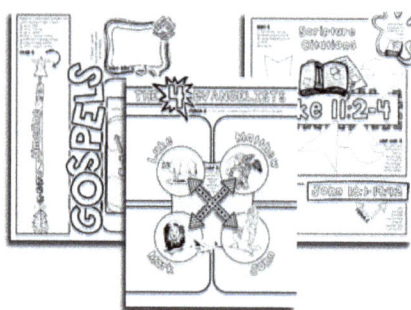

Introductory Pages
to set the stage & learn about the Gospels, meet the Evangelists, and review how to read Scripture citations

Liturgical Seasons Cover Pages
Just for fun & organization!
(Students can color if they want to)

doodle notebook

What's Included?

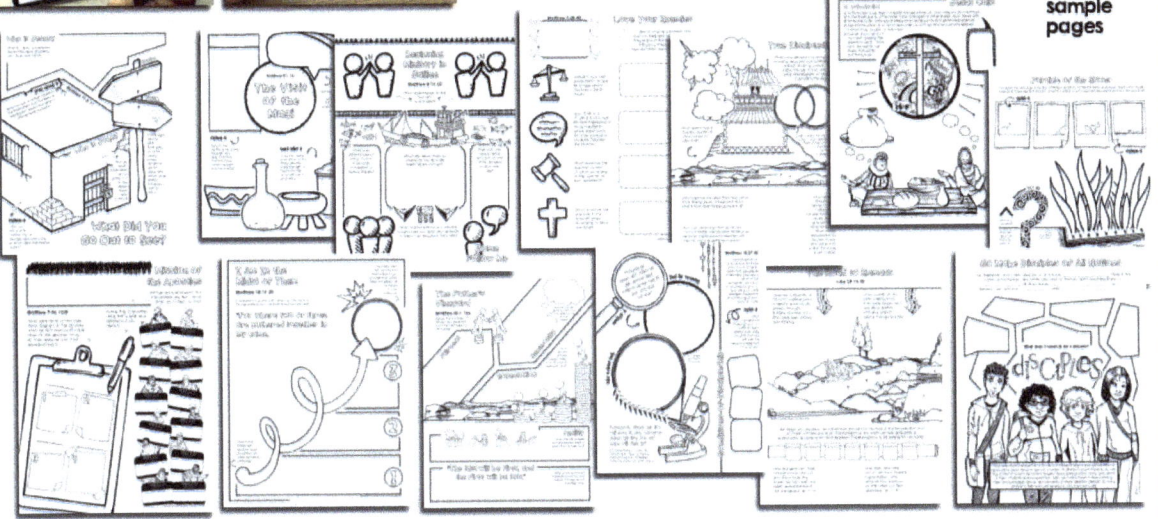

sample pages

Visual, Interactive "Doodle Note" Pages for Every Sunday Gospel
Students will doodle, color-code, sketch, reflect, color, think, and pray their way through the Gospels all year long

---

doodle notebook

What's Included?

Teacher Guides

to provide background info and reflection & discussion questions

A Blend of Factual Information and Guided Reflections

The student pages cover the details and background information, but they also provide connections to daily life and opportunities for reflection and prayer.

How to Use

Book Setup & Organization

The book is organized by liturgical season to make it easy to find each week's Gospel page, even as the liturgical calendar changes each year. This book is designed to be used with Cycle Year A, and will always work during years that follow Cycle A (every third year).

However, there will still be slight variations in the sequence of days. For example, if a Holy Day of Obligation happens to fall on a Sunday in a given year, then you may not use that particular Ordinary Time Gospel, since it is replaced with the one for that Holy Day instead.

So don't worry if you do not use a page during one year, and be aware that you will have to flip back and forth between sections in this book as you go through the seasons. For example, at one point in Ordinary Time, Lent begins and you will pause that section, flip ahead to Lent and Easter, and then go back to Ordinary Time once Easter is over.

Use the Table of Contents as a reference, and if you need additional support as you follow the liturgical calendar, the USCCB.org website is very helpful.

Bonus Pages

On the rare occasion that the Gospel that is read at mass for the week does not have a page in this book (like when a special holy day falls on a Sunday or another circumstance makes the calendar not match with any standard Gospel included here), you can use one of the bonus pages included in the back of the book. These additional doodle notes will offer your students a lesson for that day so they can still enjoy doing their doodle notes for the week. Enjoy!

While creating this book, I have prayed for you and your students who will use these pages. I hope that it works well for you and brings you and your kids closer to God as you walk through the Gospels together. I've gotten help from my wonderful team of family and friends including a priest, a seminarian, a Theology Department Head, and Catholic school teachers, all with expertise in Catholic theology. We've worked hard to make it as accurate and as helpful as possible. We've been praying for guidance as we form this content, and have also prayed for all of you who will use it. We hope you enjoy these reflections and grow spiritually from them. God bless you and your students!

How to Use

Teaching with Doodle Note Pages

Before using each page, read the Gospel passage aloud together. The Scripture citation is included on every single page to make this easy! Even if students have just heard it at mass, it is usually necessary to re-read it and have a printed copy available for them to access as a reference while they work through the pages. They can check the text as they answer questions, color, doodle, sketch, and add creative embellishments.

A wonderful website for the text of the Gospels is USCCB.org, and the version shown there is what these pages were directly based upon. However, your class set of Bibles or home Bible will do the trick too if you prefer that option.

One of the best ways to use the doodle note method is to do a teacher model. The easiest way to do this is to project/display a blank copy of the same doodle page that students have in front of them. Then, complete your "teacher copy" as you give notes. You can expand past it and add more notes on the board, talk through the lesson, and lecture as you normally would.

Even if you keep your note page "bare bones" and just fill in the blanks, your main job is to talk and model the concept and examples, just as you normally would. Students will have plenty of time to embellish their pages while you talk about the Gospel and explain more. They can also discuss it in small groups.

It can also be helpful to show completed samples to help inspire your students, at least the first few days until they get comfortable with the artistic aspect. You can save your own colored samples as you go, or collect a few student samples from previous years if you'd like. We've included a couple samples here and there to get you and your students inspired.

We recommend that you review **all** the directions on a page with the students before they begin. Sometimes they have to write or draw things in specific places. The goal is to help connect the visuals to the words in a way that helps them reflect, learn, and remember.

In any extra time, encourage students to include additional relevant doodles in the margins based on parts of the Scripture that strike them, or copy a line in creative lettering if it's something that they want to remember or pray about later.

How to Use

Teaching with Doodle Note Pages

Encourage creativity!

These pages are extremely flexible, and the best way to use them really depends on your own students and your classroom culture. Using the same page can go completely differently in your 1st period class than in your 2nd period class. Some classes will take it and run with it, and some will walk through it right alongside you as you fill it in together like a whole class graphic organizer.

There are really no "right ways" or "wrong ways" to teach with doodle notes. Be flexible, and if you would like more tips about this teaching strategy, I've got plenty of resources to help you along the way at doodlenotes.org

How to Use

Getting Started

The new Liturgical Calendar Year always begins with Advent.

The ideal time to begin this book is in the fall.

You can start with the introductory pages and cover one page per week in the three weeks **before** Advent begins if you wish. If you have more time in the fall, you can also use the Liturgical Calendar page in the "Bonus" section to review the seasons of the church year.

Then, throughout Advent, after each Sunday gospel, cover one page per week. Continue in a similar way from there on, using the book throughout the entire church year. You can use the pages each Monday if you are in a traditional classroom setting (or each Friday if you prefer to do it before the weekend Gospel and wind down for the end of the week). In a Sunday School Faith Formation class, or in a home setting, you can do these immediately after hearing the Sunday Gospel at mass.

If you are not starting in the fall, don't worry – you can just pick up wherever you are in the year. In this case, we do recommend that you go back and revisit the other pages in any free time, though. There are such wonderful lessons and reflection opportunities that can come from each different Gospel message, even if you are reading one that does not happen to correspond to the mass readings on any given day.

These visual interactive note pages offer a wonderful and relaxing way to connect with God in your own creative way as you reflect on His word. Any time that feels appropriate for a calm moment with Jesus is a great time to pull out the doodle notes.

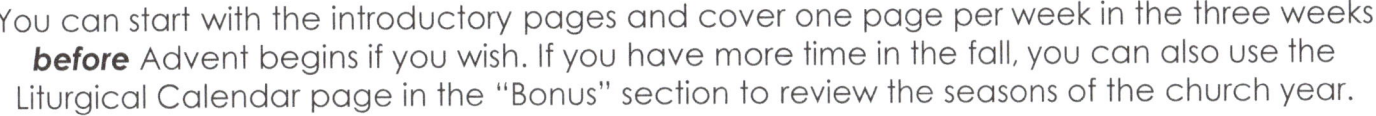

A Reminder

You may have never thought about it, but **creativity** is one of God's greatest gifts to us. When we get creative, we're using something that we have in common with God, the creator of the universe!

How amazing is it that God, who created the entire world, decided to give us each our own creativity so that we can share in one of His own greatest joys! He generously shares with us the ability to produce something beautiful!

Pass this on to your students as you invite them to use their own creativity to worship and build their own relationship with the Creator through this book. As a bonus, creating something new is also great for mental health. So, get creative!

doodle notebook

contents

Cycle Year "A"

Pages are organized by liturgical season, so you will have to flip back and forth according to the transitions between Ordinary Time and Lent, for example, since the order of the Gospels will depend on the dates for the year. Similarly, additional Holy Days of Obligation are included in their own section even though they occur throughout the calendar year because the sequence of the Gospels will vary from year to year. The USCCB website has links to the updated liturgical calendar for any given year that you can reference as needed.

Use the teacher guide that corresponds to each visual doodle note reflection page to help you lead your students through the content.

	Student Page	Teacher Guide
Introduction		
- Gospels: The Good News	14	100 (Sample: 101)
- The 4 Evangelists	15	100 (Sample: 102)
- Scripture Citations	16	103
Advent		
- First Sunday of Advent	18	106 (Sample: 107)
- Second Sunday of Advent	19	106
- Third Sunday of Advent	20	108
- Fourth Sunday of Advent	21	108
Christmas		
- Christmas Vigil	24	110
- Nativity of the Lord / Christmas Day	25	110 (Sample: 111)
- The Holy Family	26	112
- Epiphany of the Lord	27	112

contents

	Student Page	Teacher Guide
Ordinary Time		
- Baptism of the Lord (1st Sunday of O.T.)	30	114
- Second Sunday of Ordinary Time	31	114
- Third Sunday of Ordinary Time	32	115
- Fourth Sunday of Ordinary Time	33	115 (Sample: 116)
- Fifth Sunday of Ordinary Time	34	117
- Sixth Sunday of Ordinary Time	35	117
- Seventh Sunday of Ordinary Time	36	118
- Eighth Sunday of Ordinary Time	37	118 (Sample: 119)
- Ninth Sunday of Ordinary Time	38	120
- Tenth Sunday of Ordinary Time	39	120
- Eleventh Sunday of Ordinary Time	40	121
- Twelfth Sunday of Ordinary Time	41	121
- Thirteenth Sunday of Ordinary Time	42	122
- Fourteenth Sunday of Ordinary Time	43	122
- Fifteenth Sunday of Ordinary Time	44	123
- Sixteenth Sunday of Ordinary time	45	123
- Seventeenth Sunday of Ordinary Time	46	124
- Eighteenth Sunday of Ordinary Time	47	124 (Sample: 125)
- Nineteenth Sunday of Ordinary Time	48	126
- Twentieth Sunday of Ordinary Time	49	126
- Twenty-First Sunday of Ordinary Time	50	127
- Twenty-Second Sunday of Ordinary Time	51	127
- Twenty-Third Sunday of Ordinary Time	52	128
- Twenty-Fourth Sunday of Ordinary Time	53	128
- Twenty-Fifth Sunday of Ordinary Time	54	129
- Twenty-Sixth Sunday of Ordinary Time	55	129
- Twenty-Seventh Sunday of Ordinary Time	56	130
- Twenty-Eighth Sunday of Ordinary Time	57	130
- Twenty-Ninth Sunday of Ordinary Time	58	131
- Thirtieth Sunday of Ordinary Time	59	131
- Thirty-First Sunday of Ordinary Time	60	132
- Thirty-Second Sunday of Ordinary Time	61	132
- Thirty-Third Sunday of Ordinary Time	62	133
- Our Lord Jesus Christ, King of the Universe	63	133

contents

	Student Page	Teacher Guide
Lent		
- Ash Wednesday	66	136
- First Sunday of Lent	67	136
- Second Sunday of Lent	68	137
- Third Sunday of Lent	69	137 (Sample: 138)
- Fourth Sunday of Lent	70	139 (Sample: 140)
- Fifth Sunday of Lent	71	139
- Palm Sunday	72	141
- Holy Thursday	73	142
- Good Friday	74	142
Easter		
- Easter Sunday	76	144
- Divine Mercy Sunday	77	144
- Third Sunday of Easter	78	145
- Fourth Sunday of Easter	79	145
- Fifth Sunday of Easter	80	146
- Sixth Sunday of Easter	81	146
- Seventh Sunday of Easter	82	147
- Ascension of the Lord	83	147
- Pentecost	84	148
Additional Holy Days		
- Immaculate Conception	86	150
- Mary the Mother of God	87	150
- Feast of the Assumption	88	151
- All Saints Day	89	151 (Sample: 152)
Bonus Pages		
- The Armor of God	92-93	154-155
- The Liturgical Calendar	94	156-157
- Holy Week	95	158-159

INTRO TO THE GOSPELS

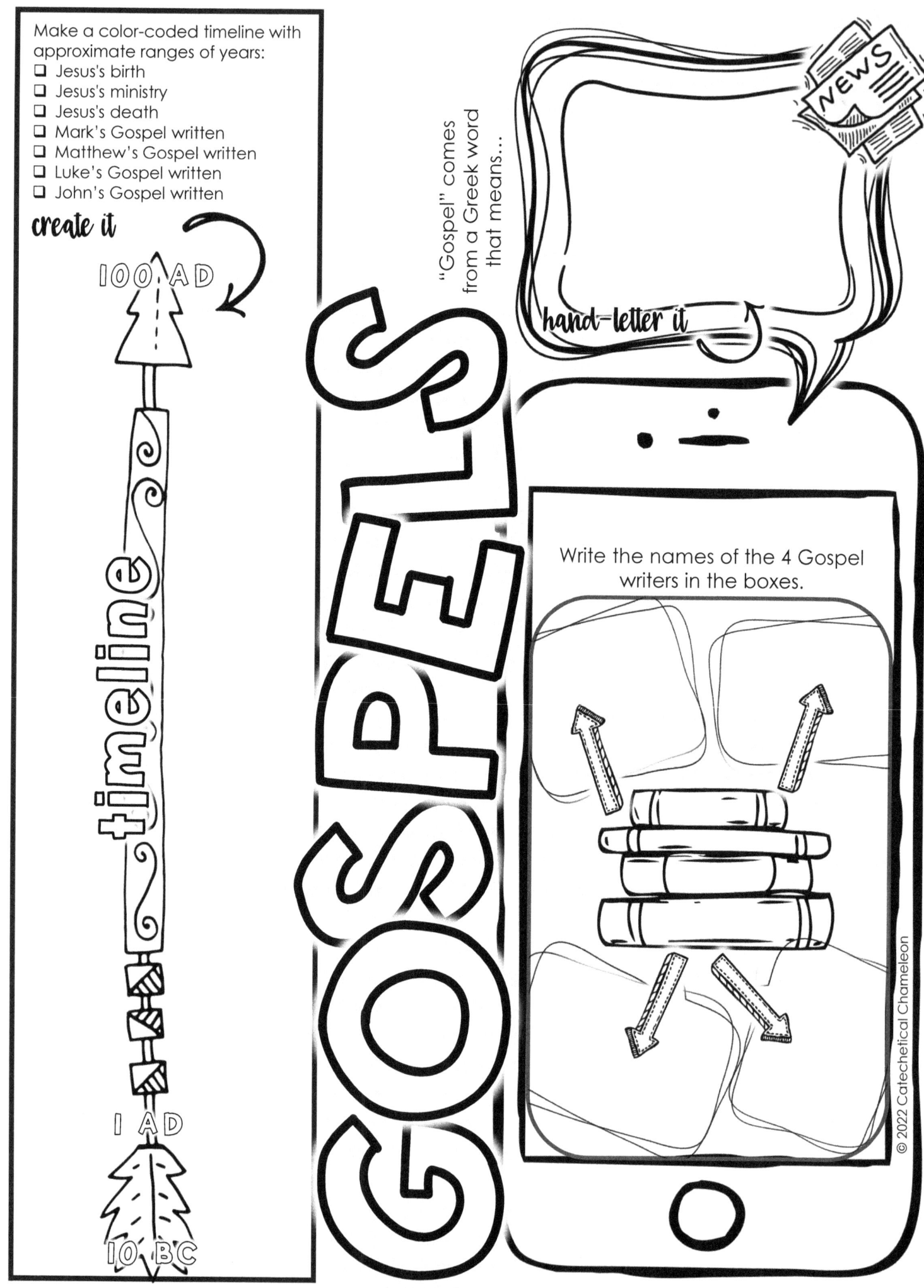

THE 4 EVANGELISTS

explain it — In the boxes, tell what is special about each evangelist.

Luke

Matthew

color it — Color the symbols, & write why each represents that writer.

© 2022 Catechetical Chameleon

Mark

John

15

Scripture Citations

label it
In the arrows, identify:
- ☐ Verse (starting line #)
- ☐ Verse (stopping line #)
- ☐ Book
- ☐ Chapter

Remember, the Bible is a collection of many _____.

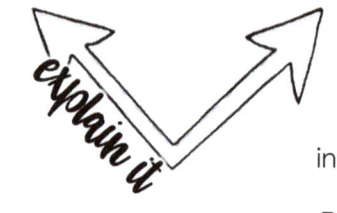

Luke 11:2-4

try it
Find this passage. What is this part of Luke's Gospel about?

color code it
Use one color for the **book** and its arrow label, another for the **chapter**, and another for the **verses**.

© 2022 Catechetical Chameleon

John 18:1-19:42

try it
Find this passage. What is this part of John's Gospel about?

explain it

(This passage continues into another chapter. Explain how to read this.)

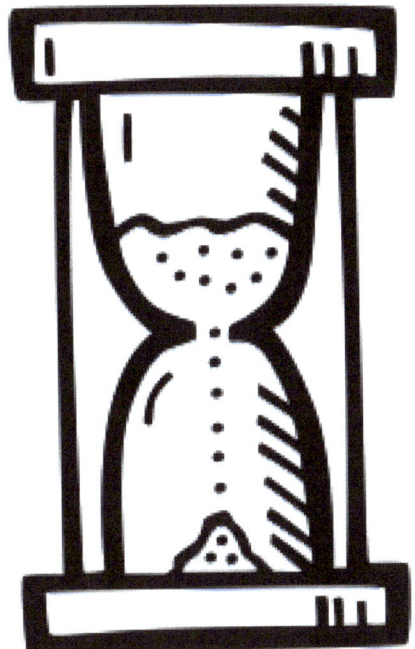

ADVENT

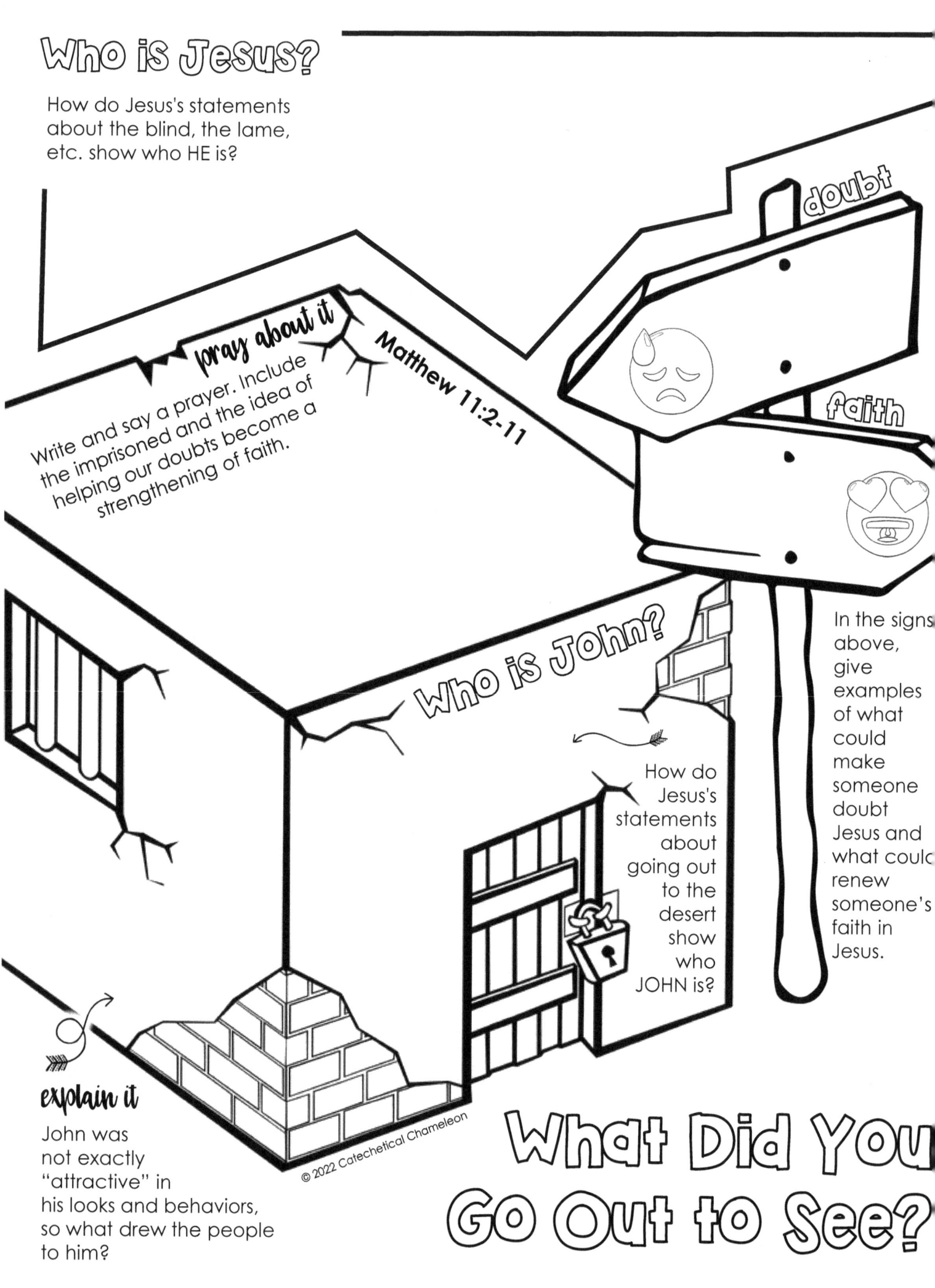

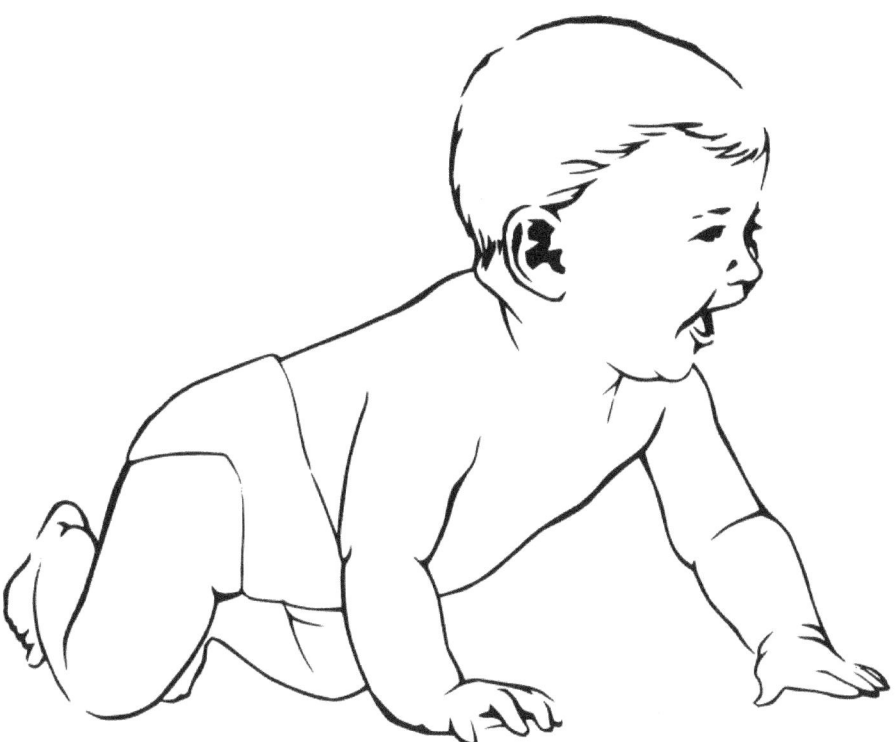

CHRISTMAS

What makes you feel safe?

Running from Herod

Matthew 2:13-15, 19-2

Create a visual story that tells about Herod's plan and Joseph's dream.

a king...

a slaughter...

...and a dream

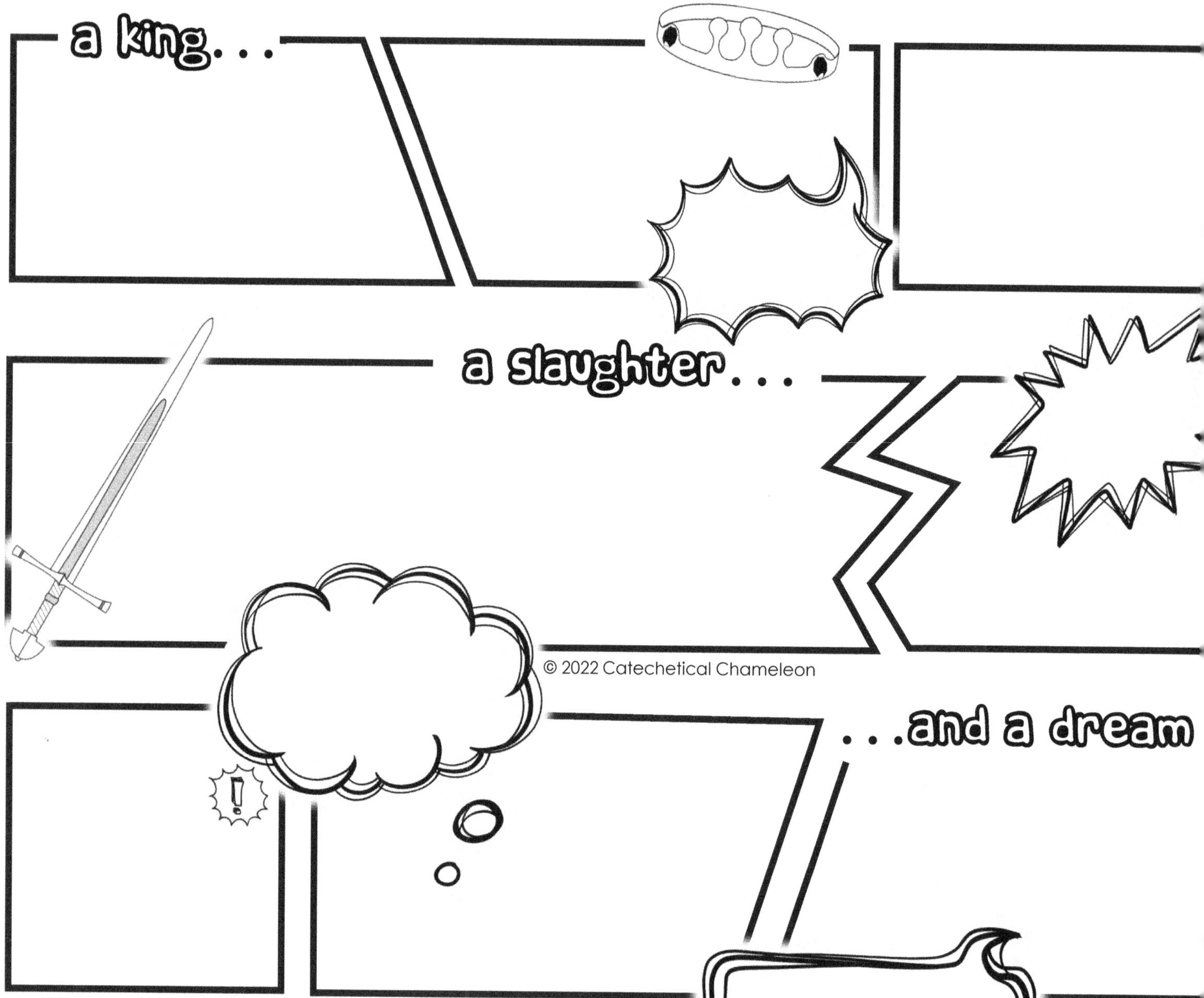

© 2022 Catechetical Chameleon

Reflect on Joseph as a protective father. Write and say a short prayer about this.

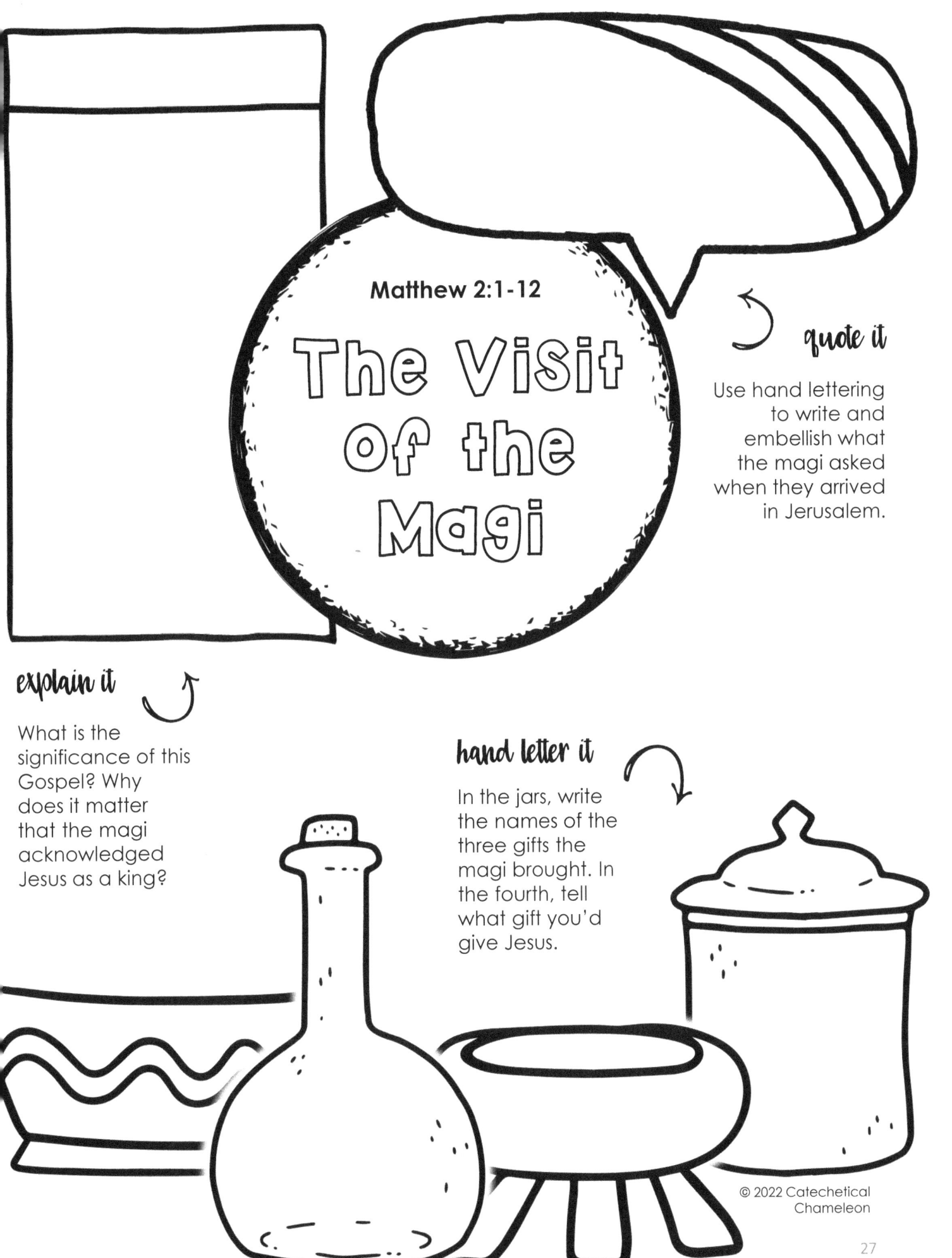

The Visit of the Magi

Matthew 2:1-12

quote it
Use hand lettering to write and embellish what the magi asked when they arrived in Jerusalem.

explain it
What is the significance of this Gospel? Why does it matter that the magi acknowledged Jesus as a king?

hand letter it
In the jars, write the names of the three gifts the magi brought. In the fourth, tell what gift you'd give Jesus.

ORDINARY TIME

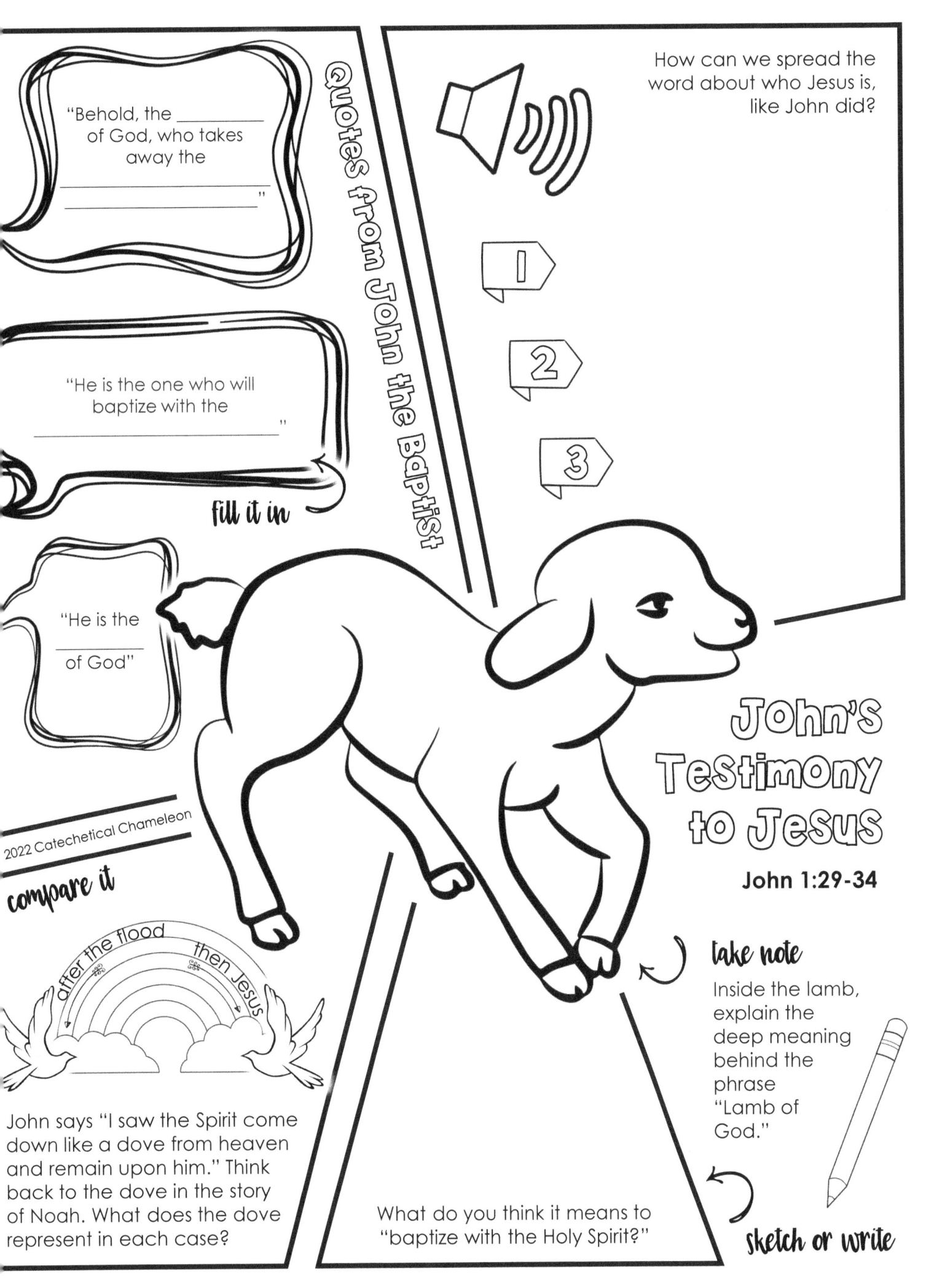

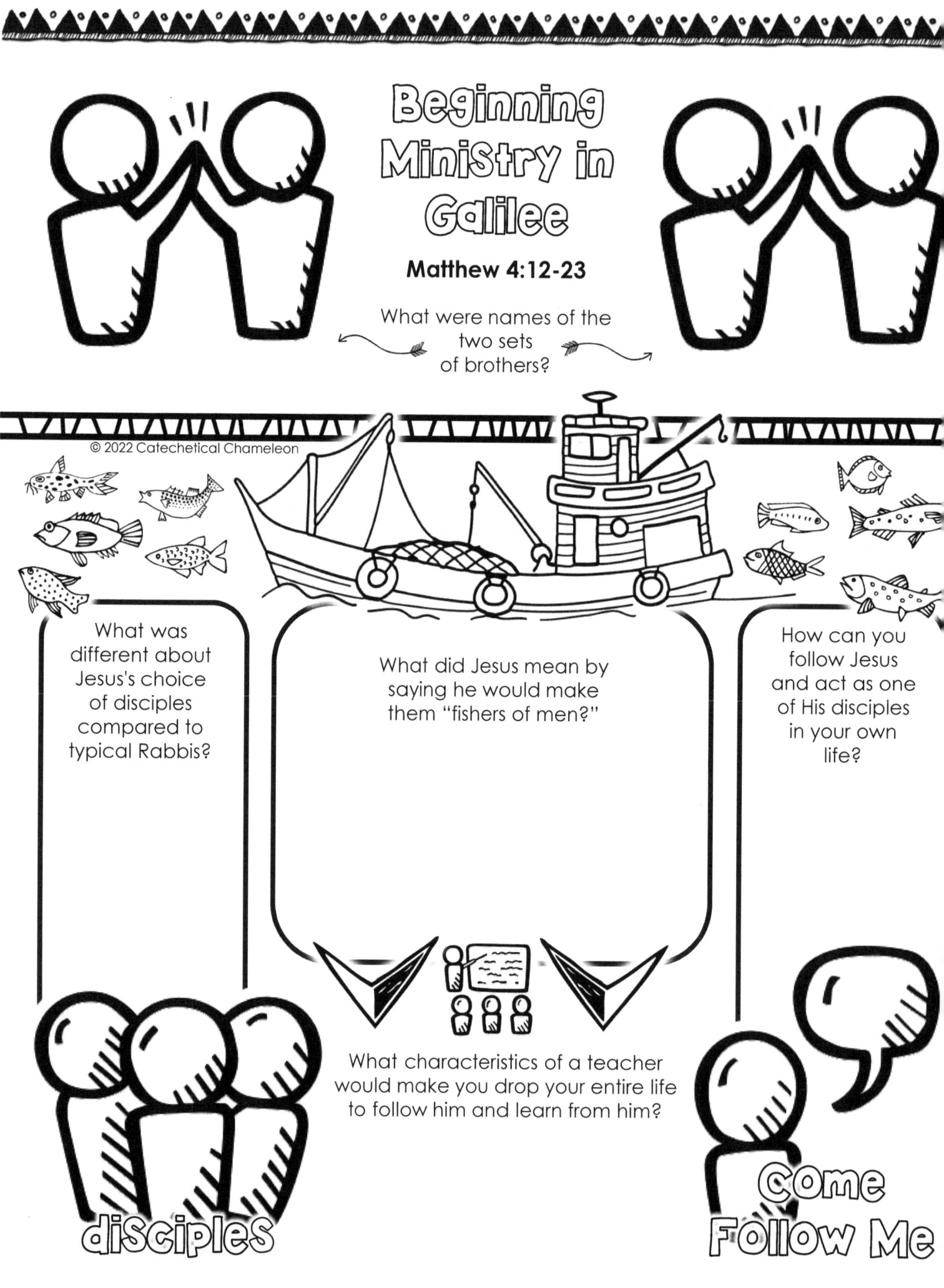

Beatitudes

Which one of these does the world need to re-think and adjust right now?

Which one of these do you need to personally reflect on?

©2022 Catechetical Chameleon

Beatitudes

Matthew 5:1-12a

In the balloon, sum up the big idea behind what Jesus is teaching in this sermon. To the right, complete each of the beatitudes.

Color code it: Color the beatitudes that you find most tricky/complicated in one color that you identify here: ⬡ and the ones that seem obvious / easy to you in another color that you identify here: ⬡

- Blessed are they who mourn
- Blessed are the poor in spirit
- Blessed are the merciful
- Blessed are they who are persecuted for the sake of righteousness
- Blessed are the meek
- Blessed are the peacemakers
- Blessed are they who hunger and thirst for righteousness
- Blessed are the clean of heart

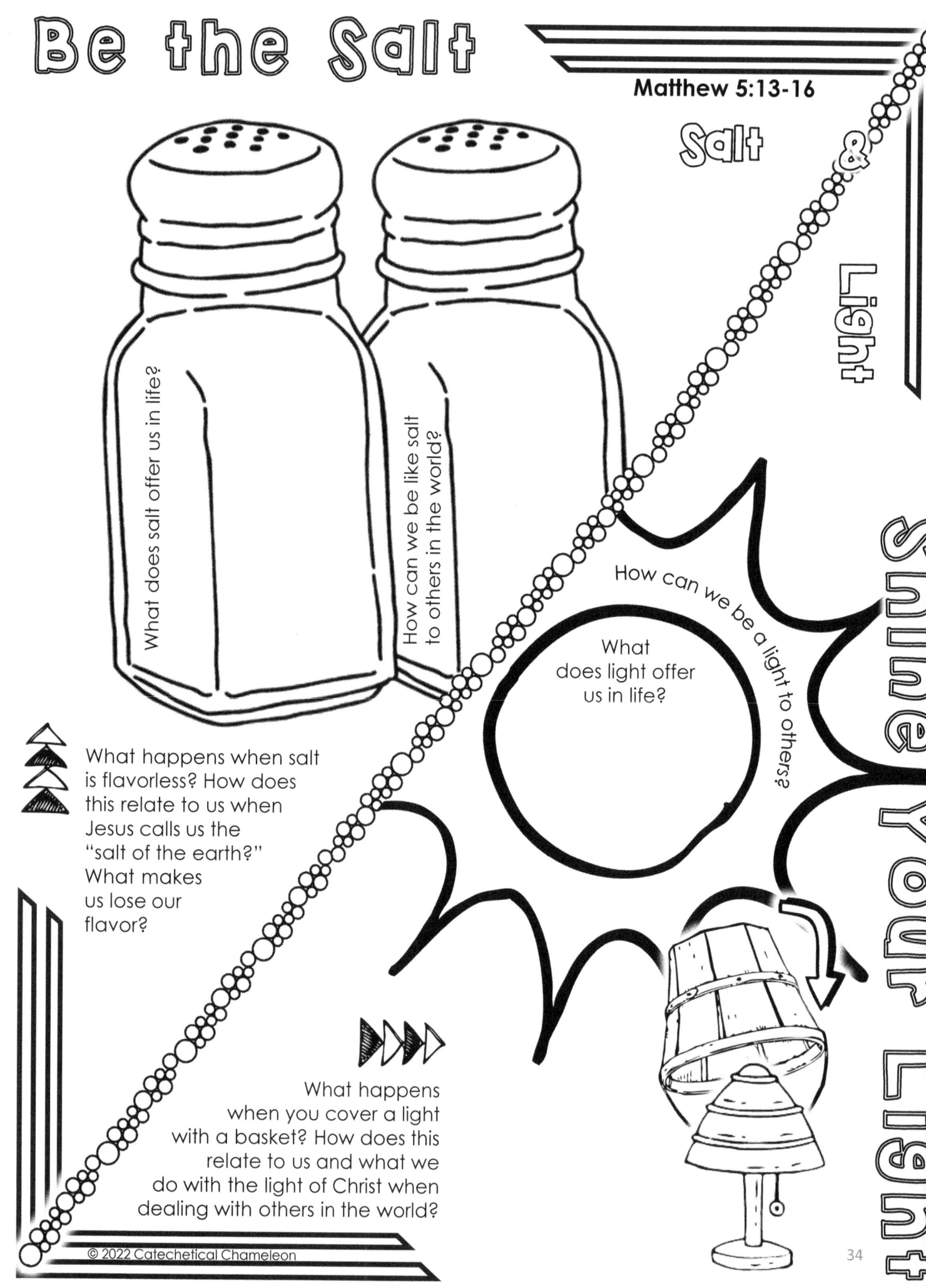

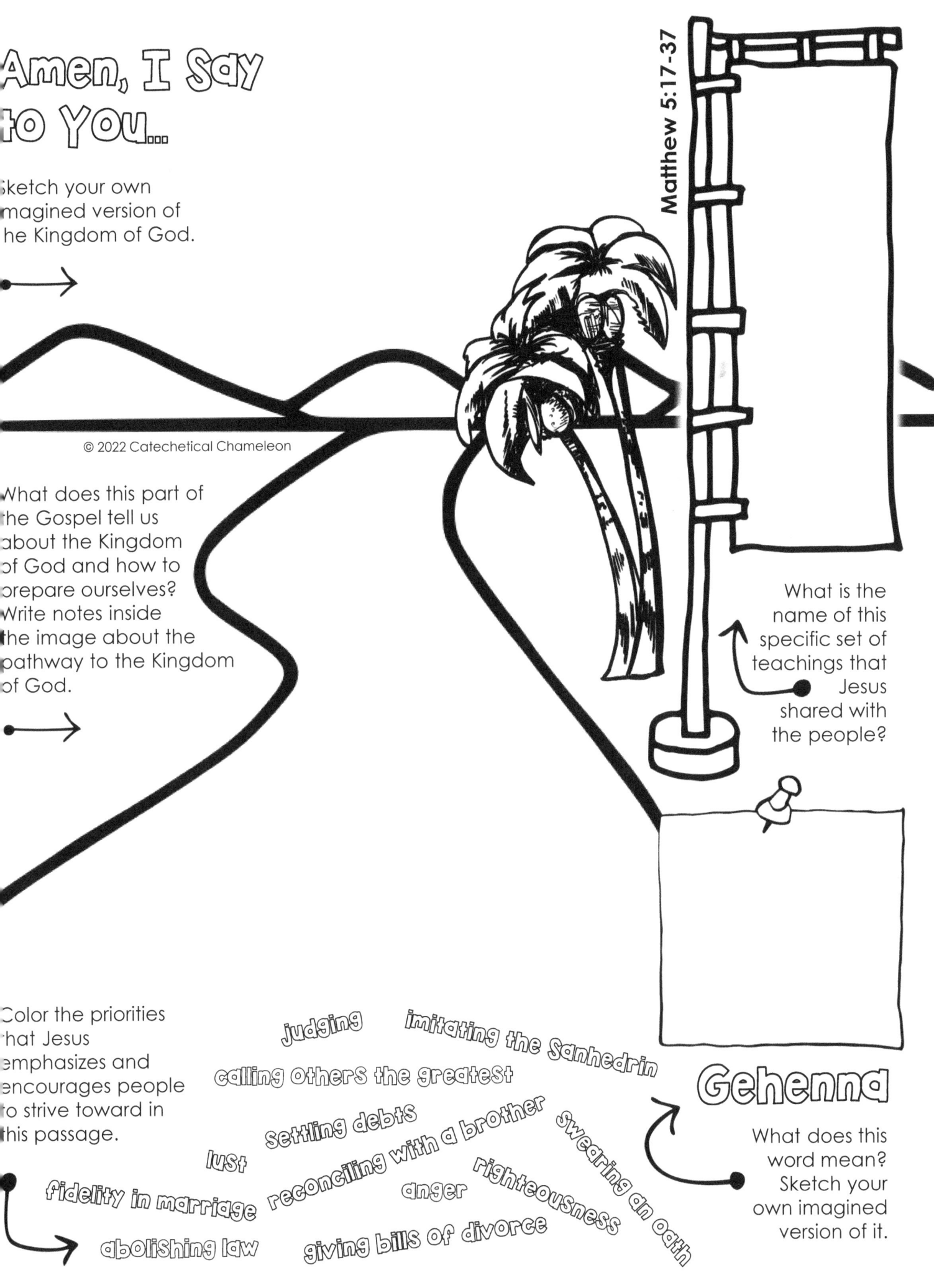

Love Your Enemies

Matthew 5:38-48

Sketch a facial expression icon that you think best represents how the people of the time reacted to this game-changing shift in the laws for which Jesus is advocating.

Explain in your own words what "an eye for an eye and a tooth for a tooth" meant.

Now, think of a situation in your own life that happened or could happen in which there would be a temptation to retaliate. Describe the situation.

What would be the response to your situation according to the "eye for an eye" guidelines?

What would be the response to the same situation according to Jesus's teaching?

© 2022 Catechetical Chameleon

Don't Worry About Tomorrow

Jesus is waiting patiently for your attention. He wants to be with you. What do you think He is saying to you if you pray and really listen?

What are the top 3 things that you give your attention to, worry about, or focus on instead of putting them in Jesus's hands and then turning your eyes to Him? Sketch those worries and distractions above.

Matthew 6:24-34

Color, Relax, Reflect, and Pray!
As you focus on this image, pray about your own worries, then make a commitment to Jesus to choose God over material things and the distractions of the world.

True Discipleship

What is the difference between truly knowing Jesus and just professing His name? What do people do to follow the will of God and then enter the kingdom of heaven? Complete the diagram.

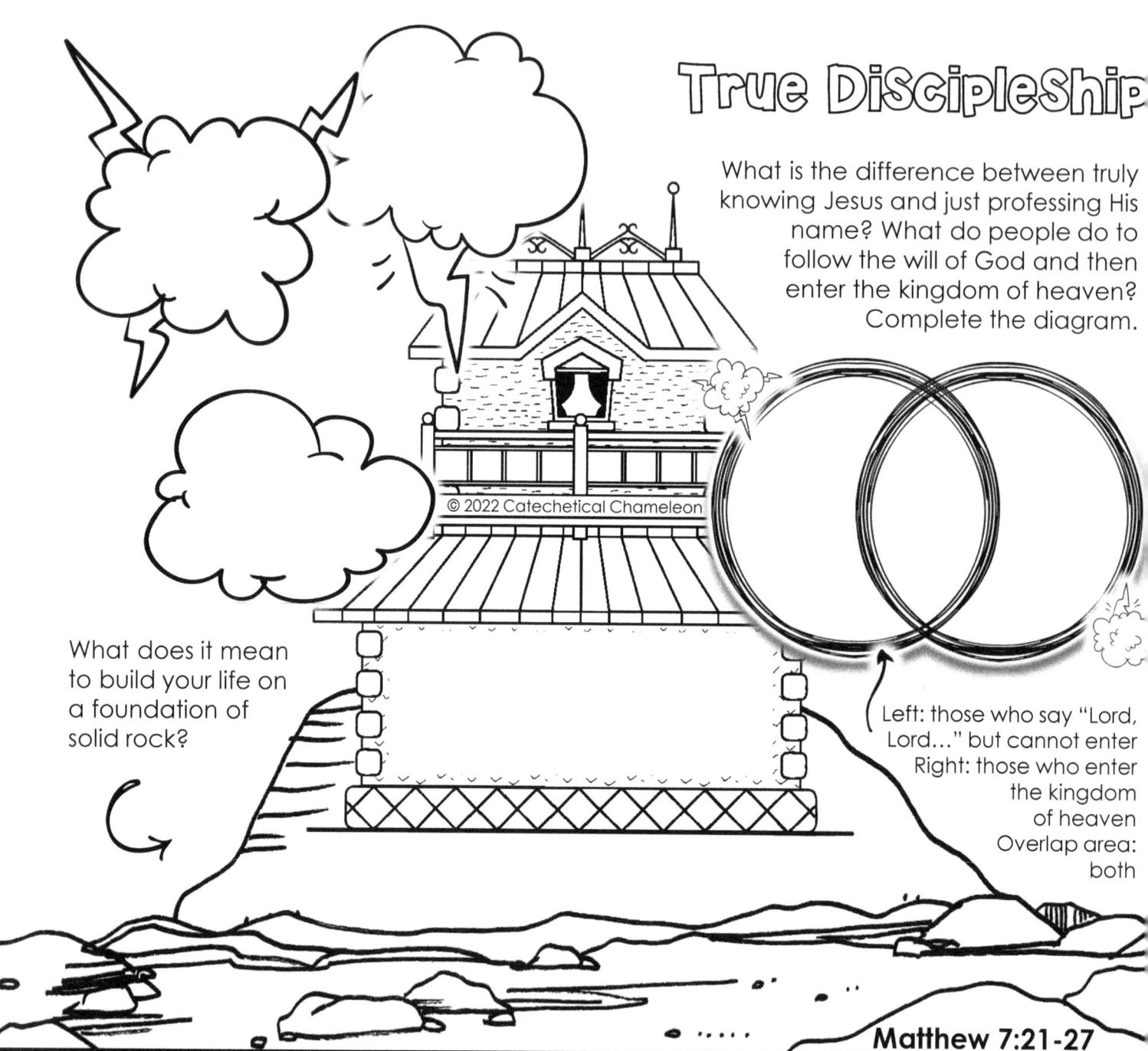

What does it mean to build your life on a foundation of solid rock?

Left: those who say "Lord, Lord..." but cannot enter
Right: those who enter the kingdom of heaven
Overlap area: both

Matthew 7:21-27

Who might be shocked that they will not enter the kingdom of heaven? What kind of lives might these people live?

How can we ensure that we do not have a horrible surprise after thinking we will enter the kingdom of heaven and then not actually getting to enter?

What kinds of things come along to try to collapse the house? Inside the clouds above, give some real life examples of what is really represented by the rain, floods, and winds that buffet the house in this Gospel.

Jesus Calls

to do(odle) list:

- In the money bag, depict/explain the reputation of a tax collector like Matthew.
- In the blank space at the table, show examples of other sinners Jesus dined with.
- Inside the foods, write words telling what eating a meal together represented.
- Around the circle, show what Jesus calls us all to do and be (use embellished handwriting, doodles, or sketches).
- Explain Jesus's quote in your own words in the speech bubble: "Those who are well do not need a physician, but the sick do."

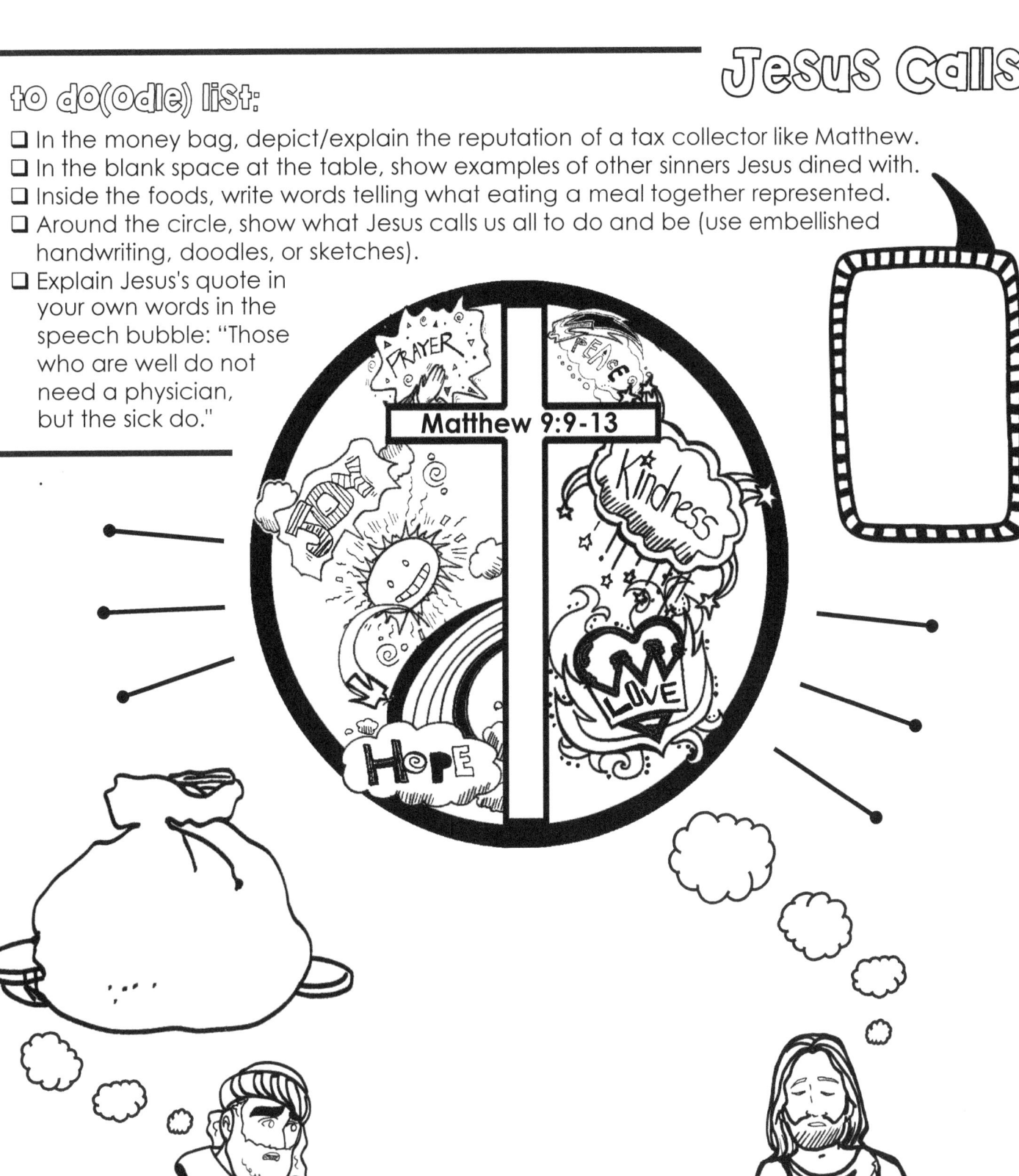

Mission of the Apostles

"The harvest is abundant, but the laborers are few." What does Jesus mean by this?

Matthew 9:36-10:8

What were some of the tasks Jesus assigned to the apostles when he sent them out? Label them on the apostles' to-do list, then draw an icon that represents each.

Name the 12 apostles, using the Gospel as a reference if you need it.

© 2022 Catechetical Chameleon

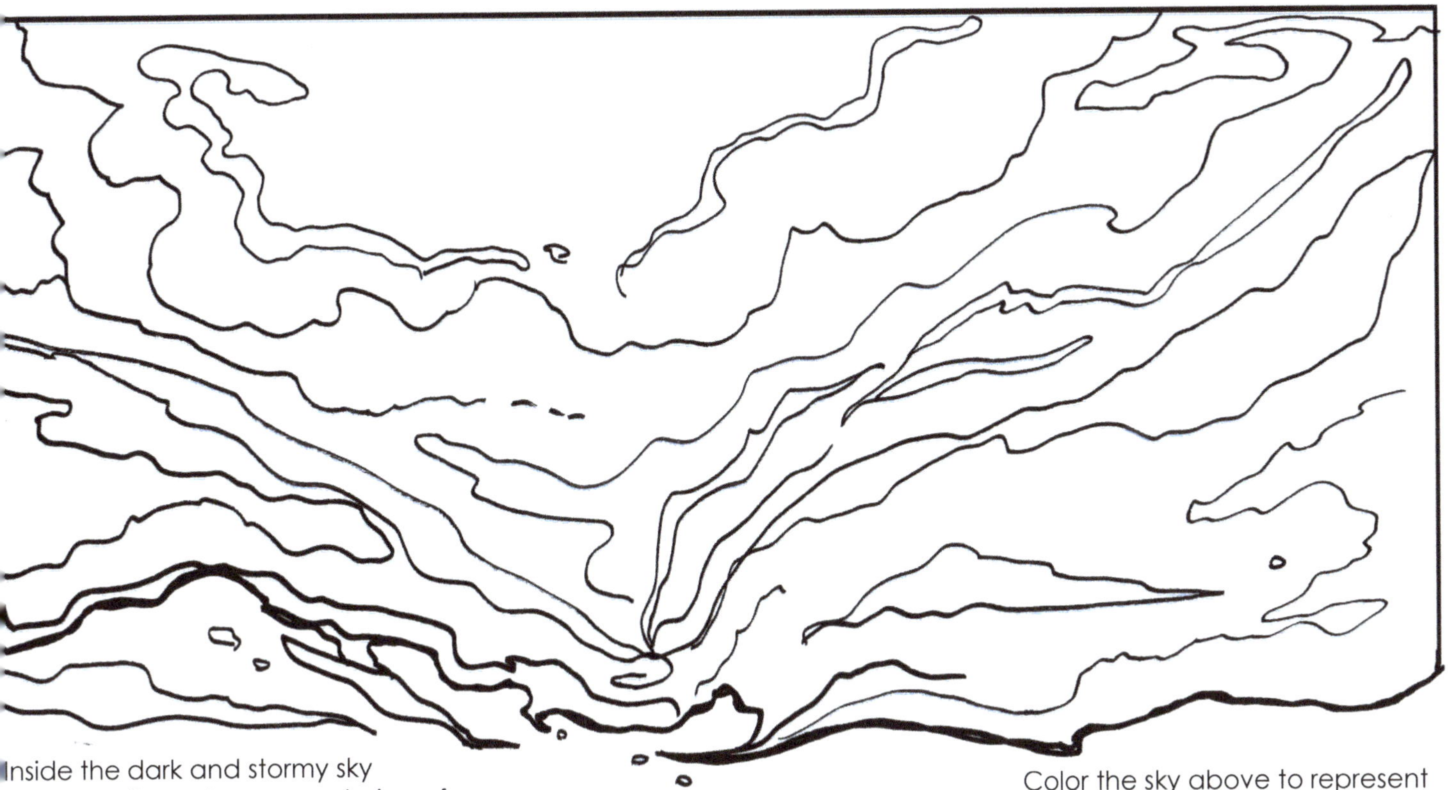

Inside the dark and stormy sky above, write or draw your choice of the following options:
- Things that are concealed that you hope God with reveal
- What is in the darkness that needs God's light
- Fears that you need to hand over to God and set aside

Color the sky above to represent darkness, fear, and concealed evil. Then, reflect and pray. How can you obey Jesus's command to not be afraid? Write a short prayer and/or poem in the blank spaces on this page, focusing on the fact that every hair on your head is counted. You're precious to God and protected by Him.

1 > What are some fears that we can tend to focus on that are only scary to the physical body?

2 > What are more important fears that concern matters of the soul?

Do Not Be Afraid

Matthew 10:26-33

Do not be afraid of those who kill the body but cannot kill the soul; rather, be afraid of the one who can destroy both soul and body in Gehenna.

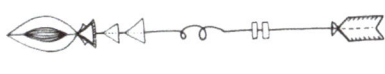

Who/what is this part about?

© 2022 Catechetical Chameleon

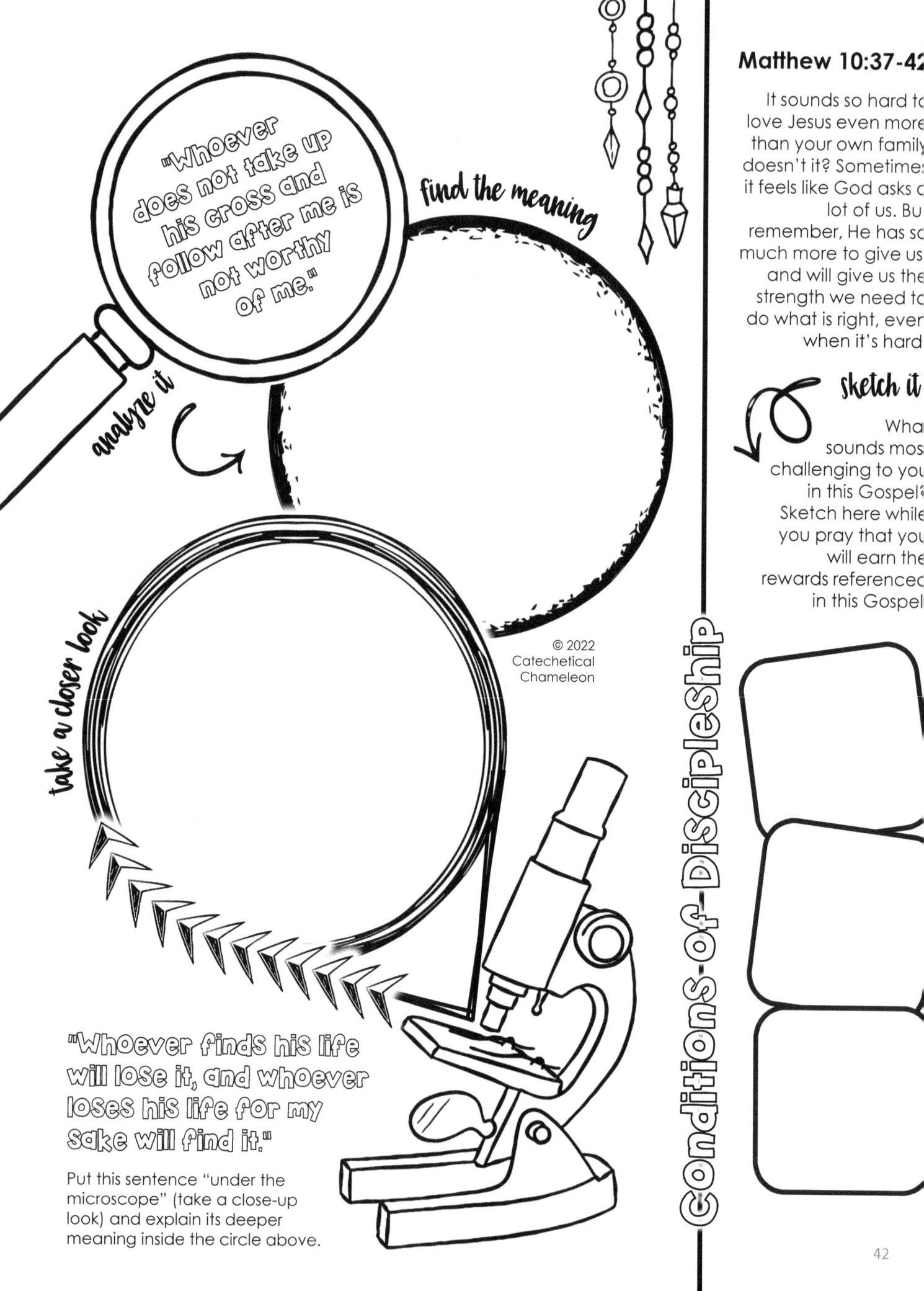

Conditions of Discipleship

Matthew 10:37-42

It sounds so hard to love Jesus even more than your own family, doesn't it? Sometimes it feels like God asks a lot of us. But remember, He has so much more to give us and will give us the strength we need to do what is right, even when it's hard.

find the meaning

"Whoever does not take up his cross and follow after me is not worthy of me."

analyze it

take a closer look

"Whoever finds his life will lose it, and whoever loses his life for my sake will find it."

Put this sentence "under the microscope" (take a close-up look) and explain its deeper meaning inside the circle above.

sketch it

What sounds most challenging to you in this Gospel? Sketch here while you pray that you will earn the rewards referenced in this Gospel.

© 2022 Catechetical Chameleon

Jesus says these things are hidden from the wise and learned. Inside the first (hidden) window, write what people He is referring to here. But then He says these things will be revealed to the childlike. In the second (clear) window, write what makes someone childlike enough to understand God and his will.

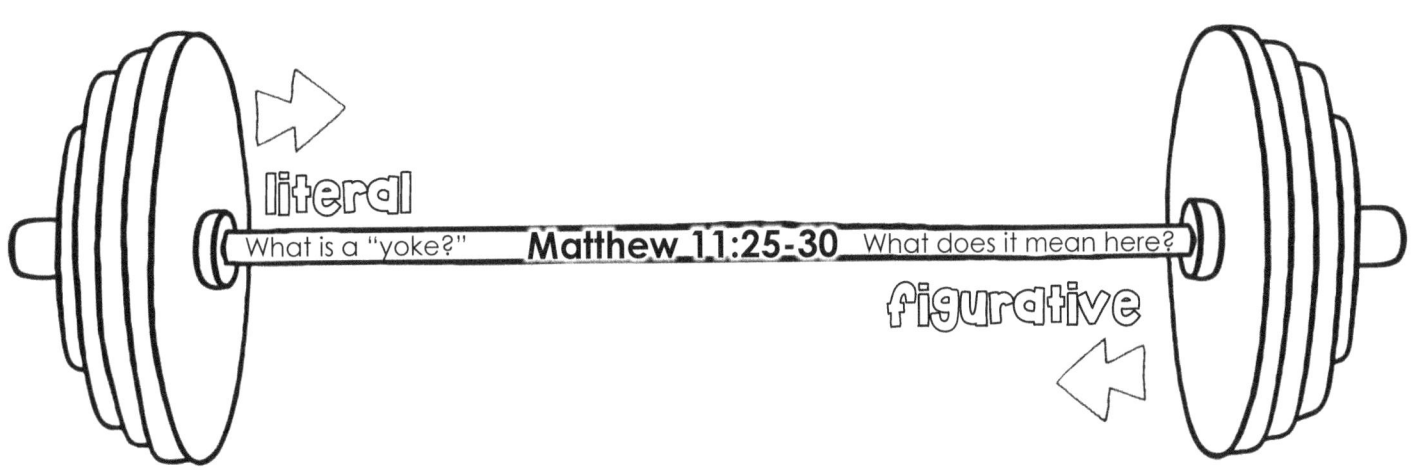

literal — What is a "yoke?" — Matthew 11:25-30 — What does it mean here? — figurative

Come to Me

Think for a while about lines 28-30 in this Gospel. After you reflect on this, and pray for a moment about it, show in words or images here what God is saying to you in these verses.

 What is the difference between being childish and childlike?

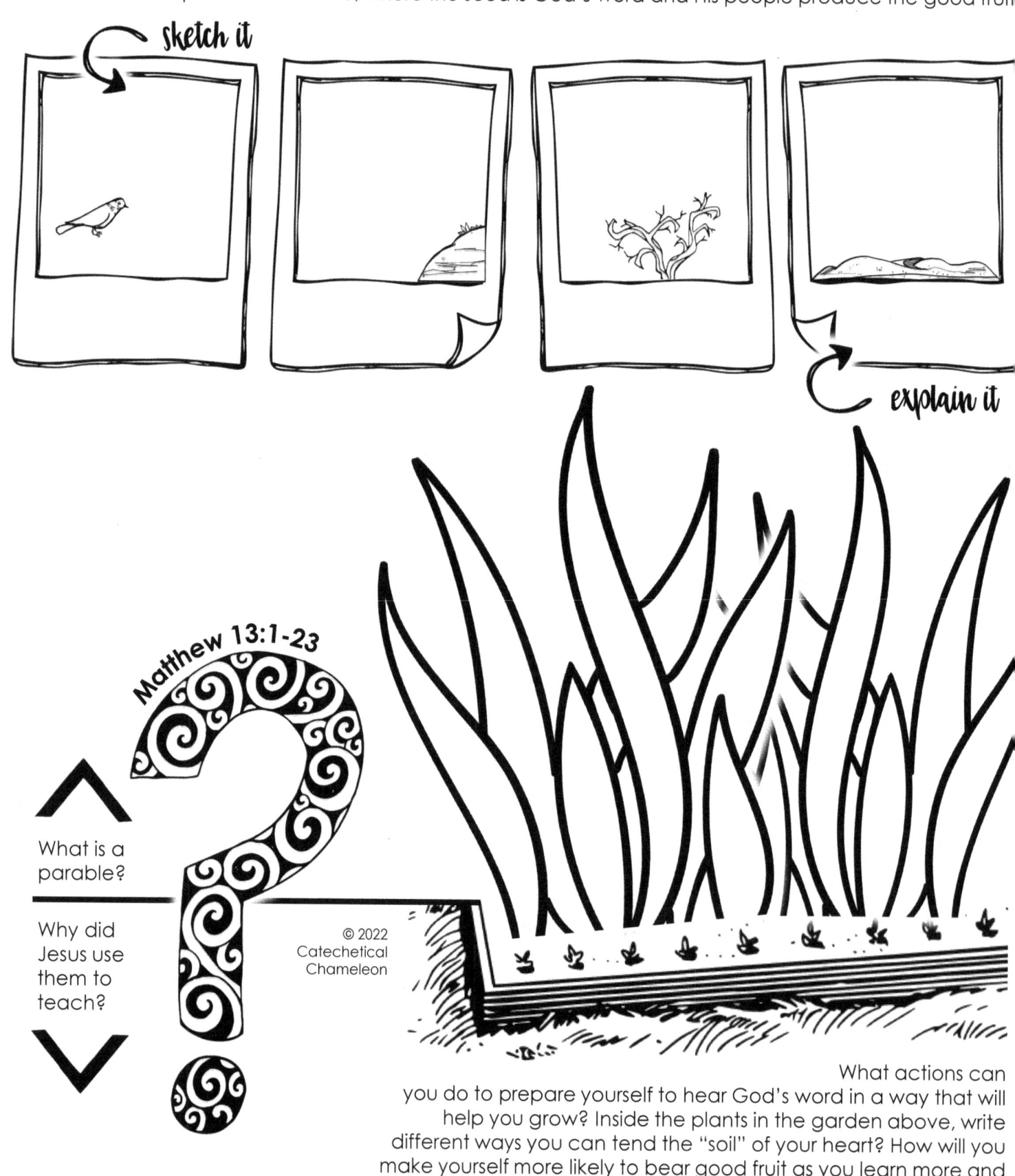

Parable of Wheat and Weeds

© 2022 Catechetical Chameleon

Matthew 13:24-43

In each image (and/or the blank space in each area), answer the question or doodle your responses.

What do the weeds represent?

Who is the enemy?

It can be discouraging to see the weeds being allowed. But remember, in the end they will get burned. In the meantime, reflect on how God can make good come from even the worst situations. He can take what the enemy intends for bad and turn it into good. Where have you seen this in your own life? Has a hardship caused some growth or goodness? Discuss with a friend.

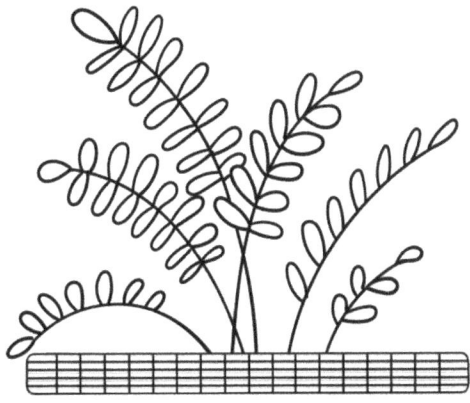

What does the story of the mustard seed represent? How does this relate to the kingdom of heaven?

Parables about the Kingdom

Write the 3 analogies Jesus uses to describe the precious treasure that is the kingdom of heaven, then make up 2 of your own in a similar way.

Make a treasure map to get to heaven! Draw it, write it, or draft up a flowchart. Use your creativity to show how the route to the amazing treasure of heaven would look in a treasure map format below. What milestones along the pathway would someone come across? What obstacles would someone face on the journey as they follow the treasure map? What lies at the destination, where x marks the spot?

At the end of the maze, doodle a representation of the kingdom of heaven.

end

start

Matthew 13:44-52

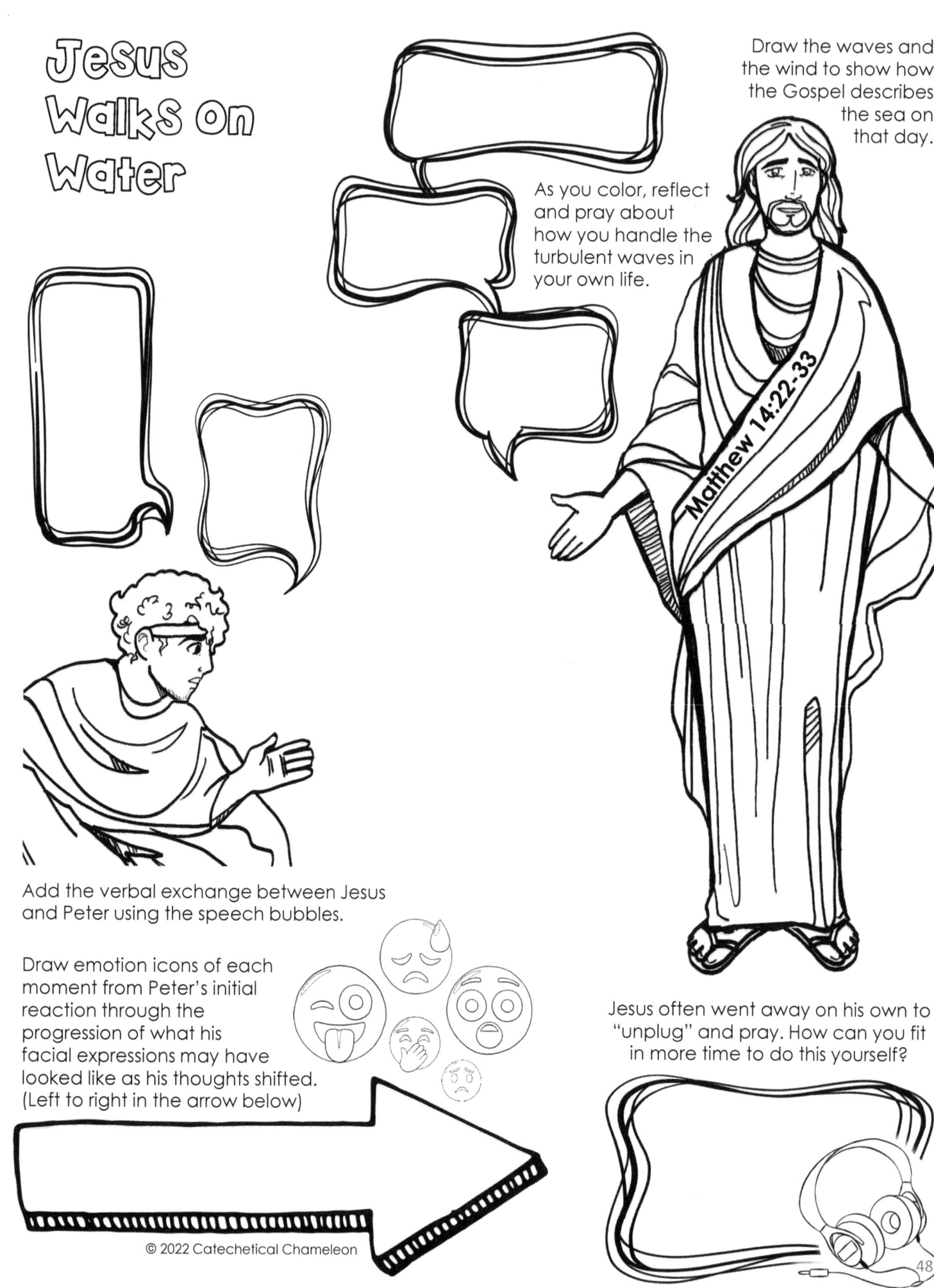

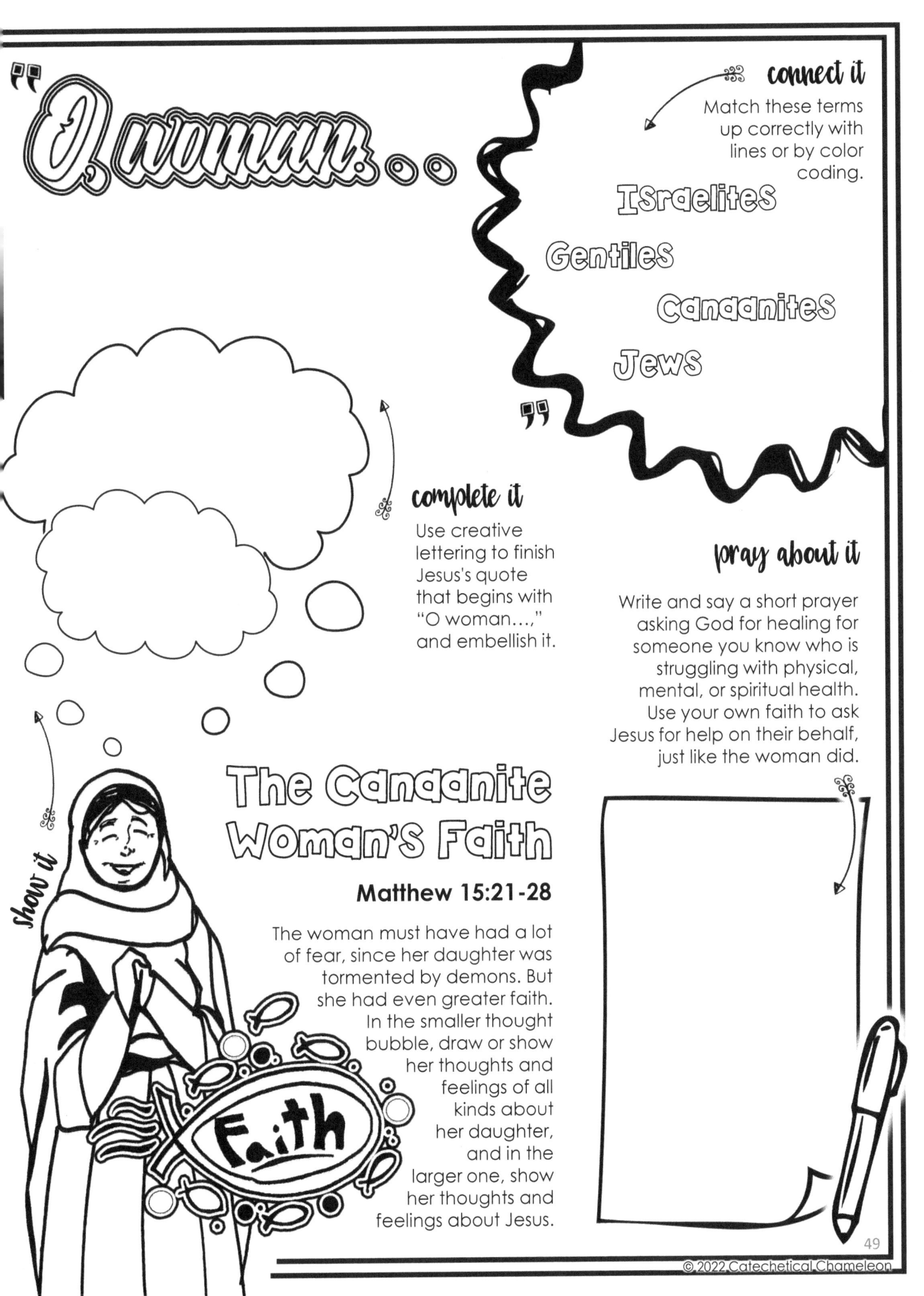

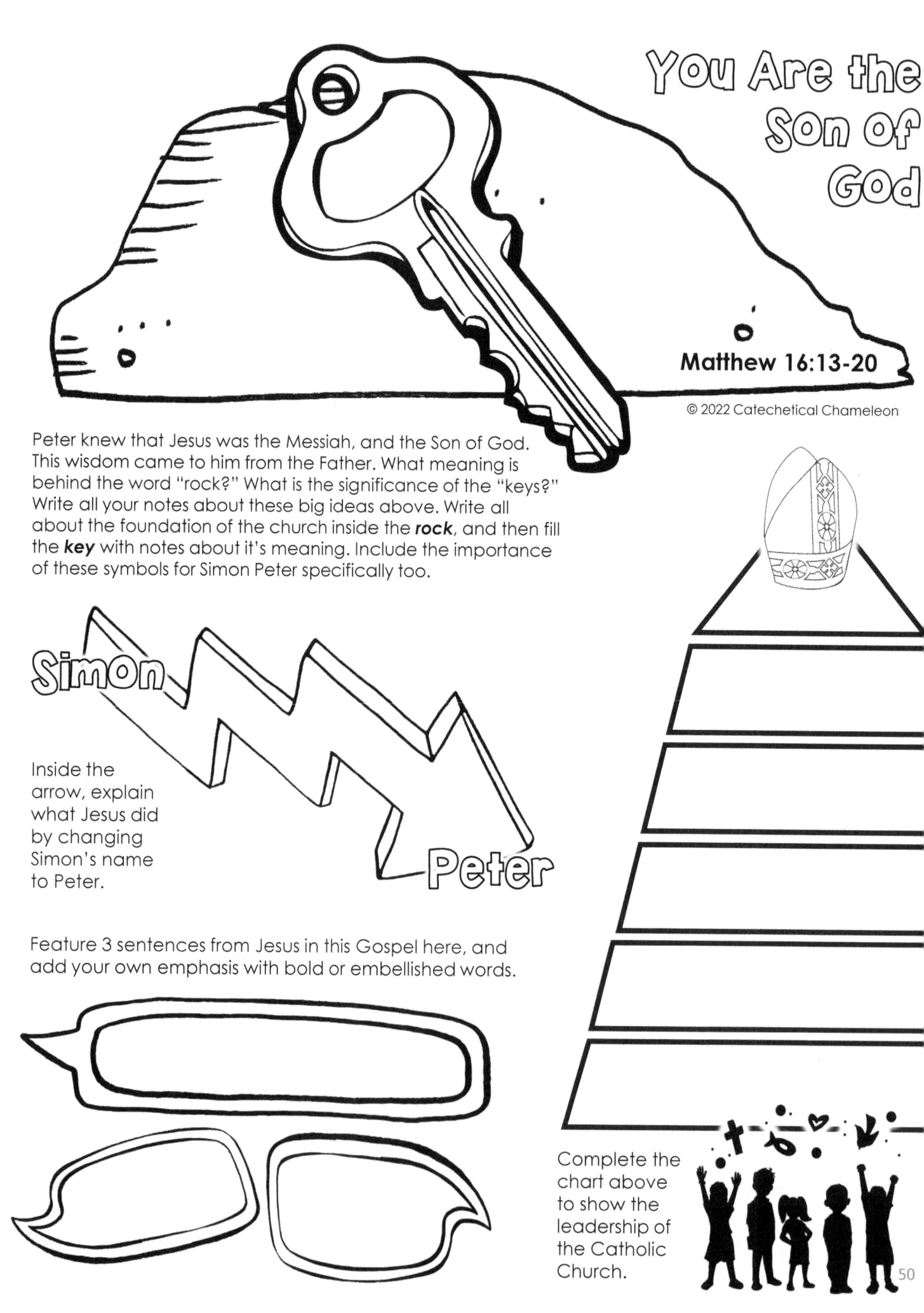

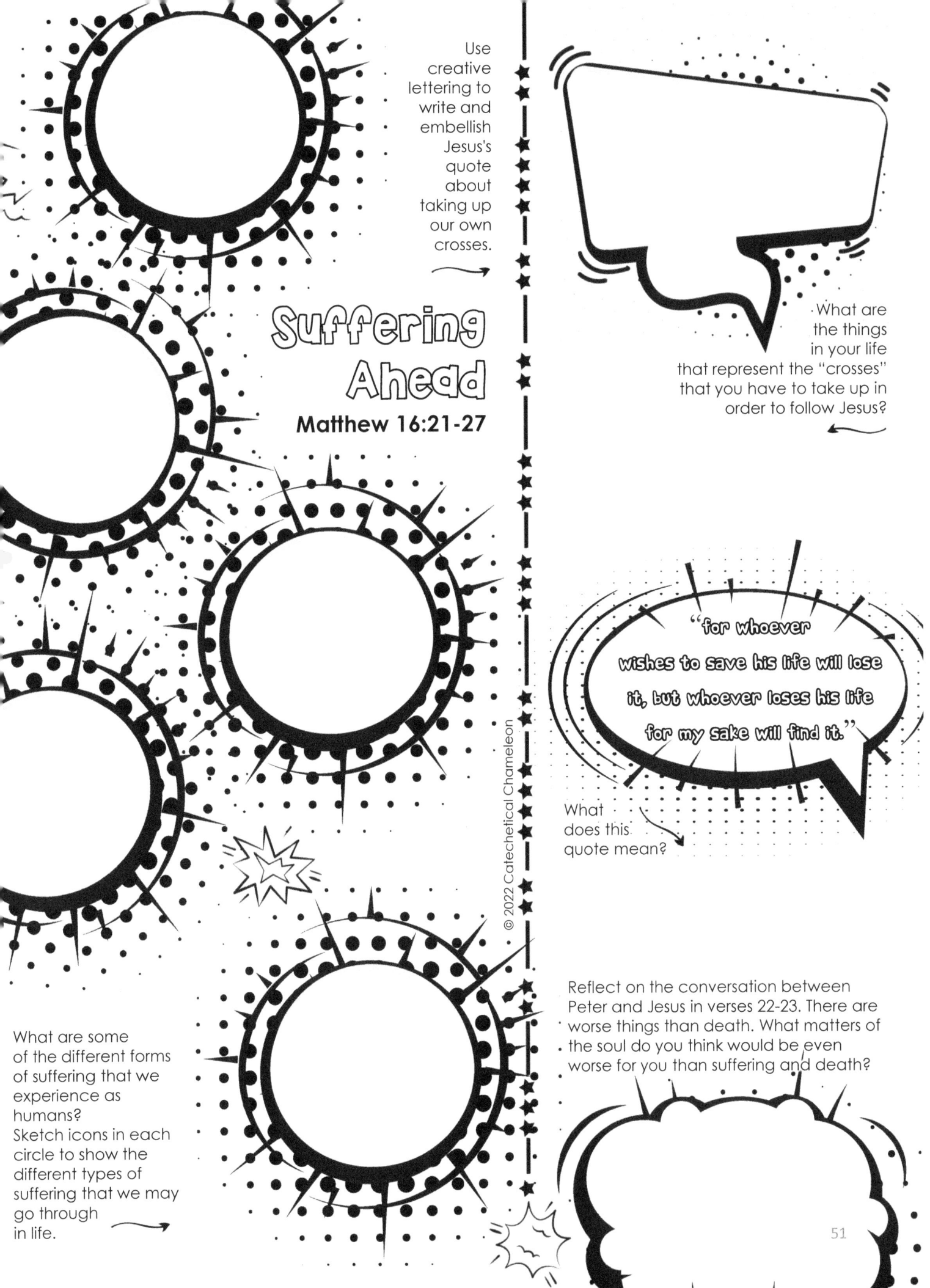

Matthew 18:21-35

Give it a title here.

Draw the story from this parable. (Stick figures are fine!)

The Unforgiving Servant

Now imagine the master as God and the unforgiving servant as yourself. What does this show you about mercy?

© 2022 Catechetical Chameleon

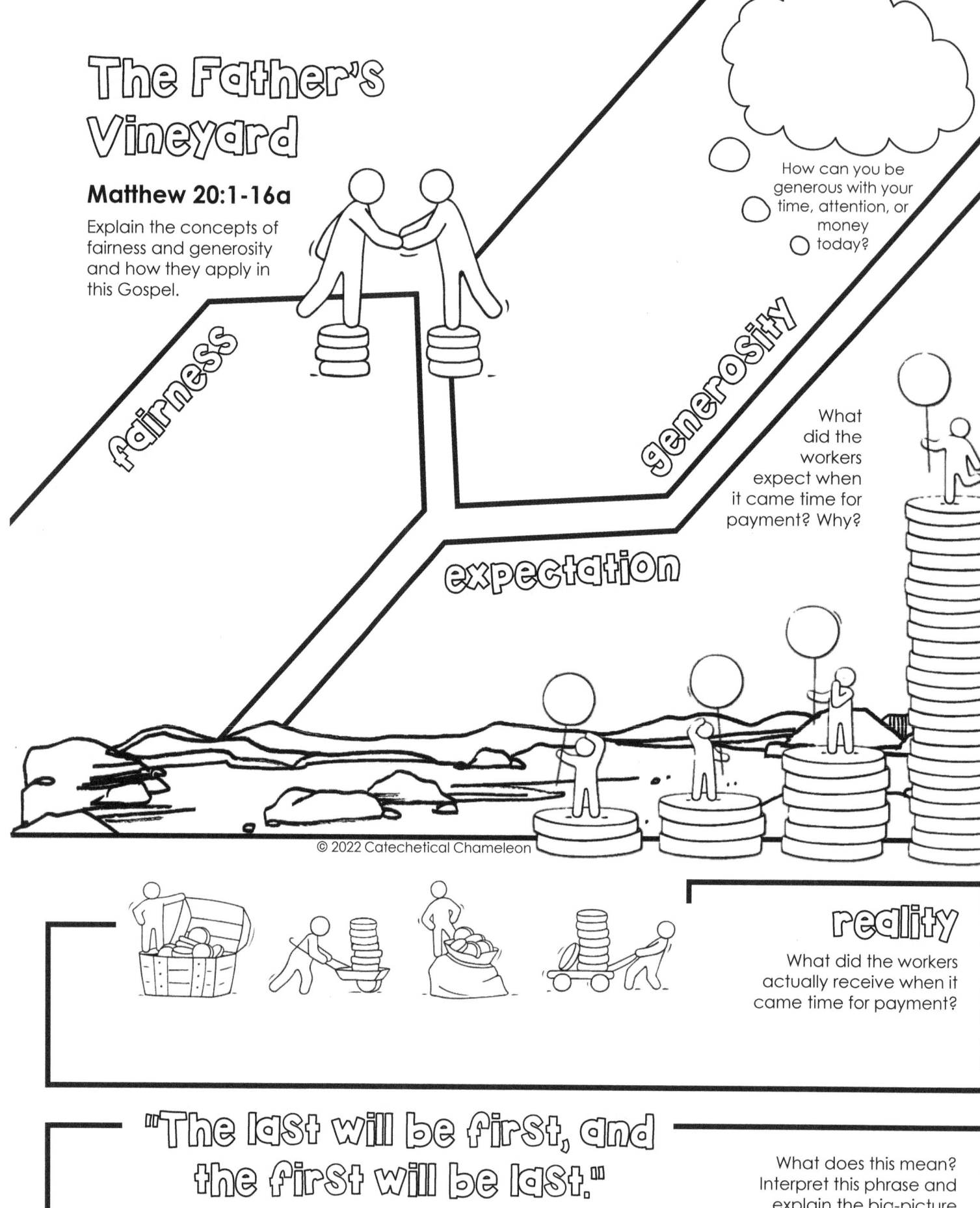

The Parable of the Two Sons

Imagine two people of Jesus's time. One is a priest who everyone sees as holy, but he does not have true faith, and is sinful behind the scenes without repenting. Another is a tax collector who everyone knows has been sinful in the past and has a bad name, but he repents and has strong faith. Draw and label both, and include in the image some things they each may say/do/think.

© 2022 Catechetical Chameleon

Matthew 21:28-32

Now imagine two people of our own time. Do a similar comparison. Who is someone who looks perfect on the outside but does not truly follow Christ? Who is someone who is strong in faith and may be more likely to "enter the kingdom of God before" the other, even if it would surprise onlookers? Draw and label both, and include in the image some things they each may say/do/think.

It's not our place to judge others or what is in their souls. Write and say a short prayer about this Gospel.

The Tenants of the Vineyard

Matthew 21:33-43

Show the story from the Gospel. (Stick figures are fine!)

Explain the meaning of the story and this key quote as it represents the way God gives the kingdom of heaven.

'the stone that the builders rejected has become the cornerstone; by the lord has this been done, and it is wonderful in our eyes' therefore, i say to you, the kingdom of god will be taken away from you and given to a people that will produce its fruit.

The Parable of the Wedding Feast

Write an invitation to the Kingdom of Heaven. What might be a good representation of the details on it? Then, complete the RSVP card and decorate it with imagery of what this feast will be like.

you're invited

r.s.v.p.

☐ yes
☐ no

© 2022 Catechetical Chameleon

Matthew 22:1-14

Reflect on people who would RSVP "no." Why do you think they might? What about people who RSVP "yes" and then have to prepare to show up? What are those preparations like?

The Greatest Commandment

Use creative lettering to write the greatest commandment.

How can you fully love God with each of these differently? What does it truly mean to Love the Lord with ALL your heart, ALL your soul, and ALL your mind? Explain.

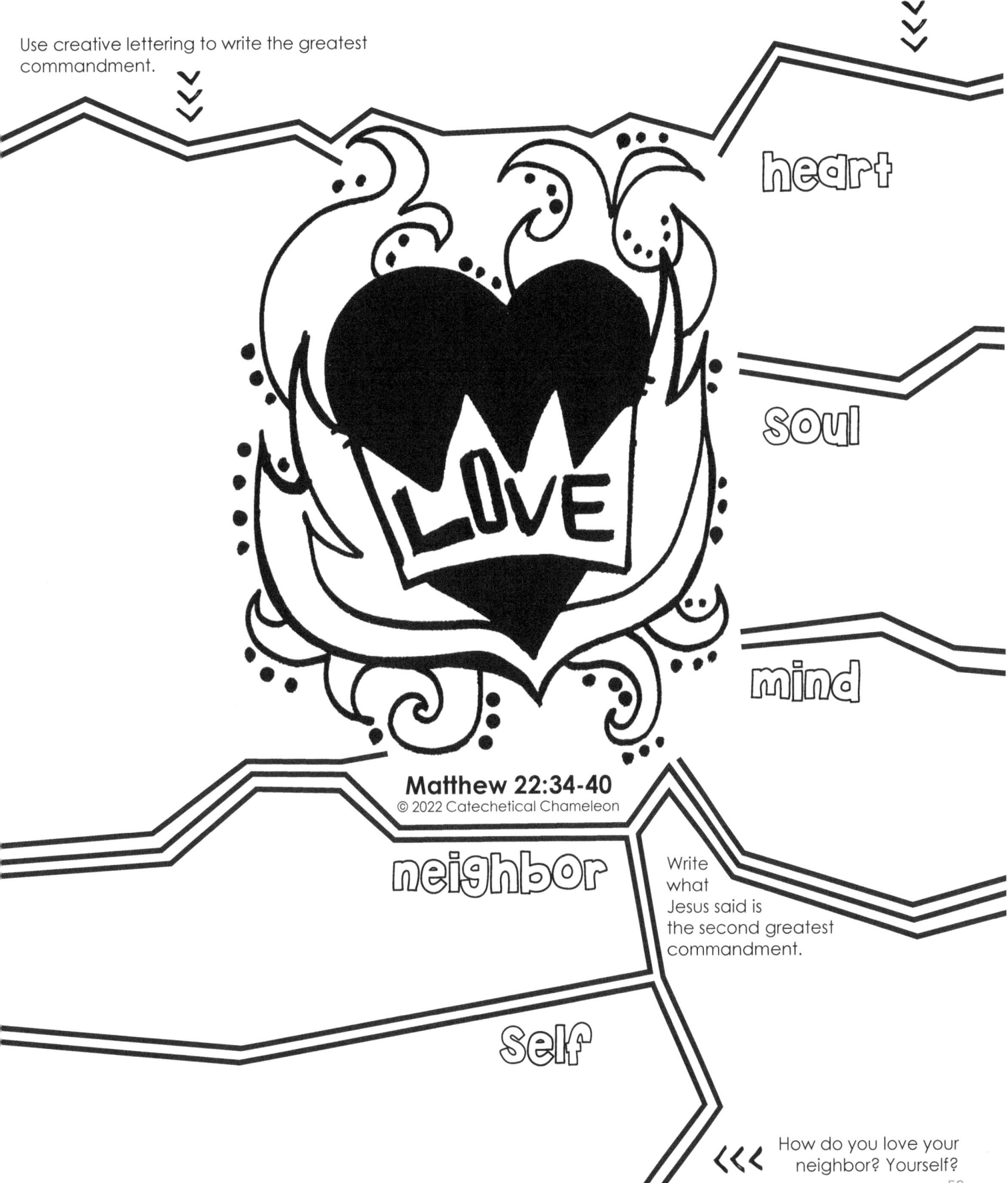

Matthew 22:34-40
© 2022 Catechetical Chameleon

heart

soul

mind

neighbor

self

Write what Jesus said is the second greatest commandment.

How do you love your neighbor? Yourself?

Whoever Humbles Himself

Matthew 23:1-12
© 2022 Catechetical Chameleon

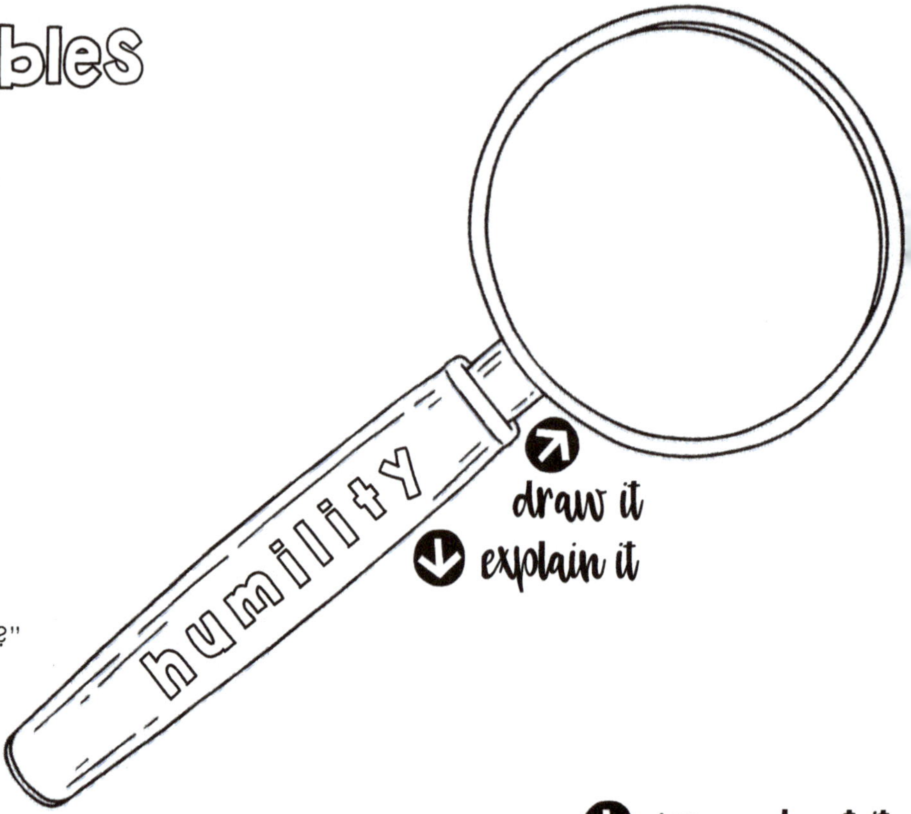

Where do you see leaders today who are hypocritical?

humility — draw it / explain it

What are your thoughts when you see someone doing something all "for show?"

pray about it

Write and say a prayer asking God to help you to live as Jesus explains here. Incorporate phrasing from the Gospel, including the following words & phrases in a similar context:
- ☑ Master
- ☑ Servant
- ☑ Greatest
- ☑ Honor
- ☑ Follow their example
- ☑ Heavy burdens
- ☑ Exalt

What are 3 ways you can serve others in a way that you are humbled instead of exalted?

Parable of the 10 Virgins

Matthew 25:1-13
© 2022 Catechetical Chameleon

Some fell asleep and ran out of oil. What does this represent? Explain inside the sleeping icon.

What does it mean here to "stay awake?" What does it look like for us to be awake and ready? Explain inside the awake icon.

Use all the empty space around this page to explain the meaning of "you know neither the day nor the hour" in words and/or doodles. Add color!

61

The Parable of the Talents

Matthew 25:14-30

What are your own talents that God has given you? What comes naturally to you? Draw 3 or 4 thick stems of a plant coming from the dirt, and label them with 3 or 4 of your talents.

How can you help these grow? What do you do to build upon your skills? Add a large leaf to each stem, and write how you can grow/build that particular talent inside the leaf.

How can you use these talents to serve God and others? Add a fruit or a flower for each, and write or draw inside each fruit or flower how you can use that talent for God's kingdom.

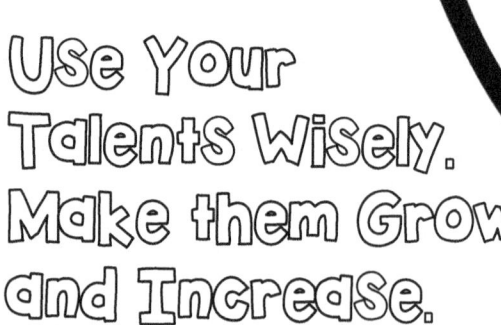

Use Your Talents Wisely. Make them Grow and Increase. Don't hide them away.

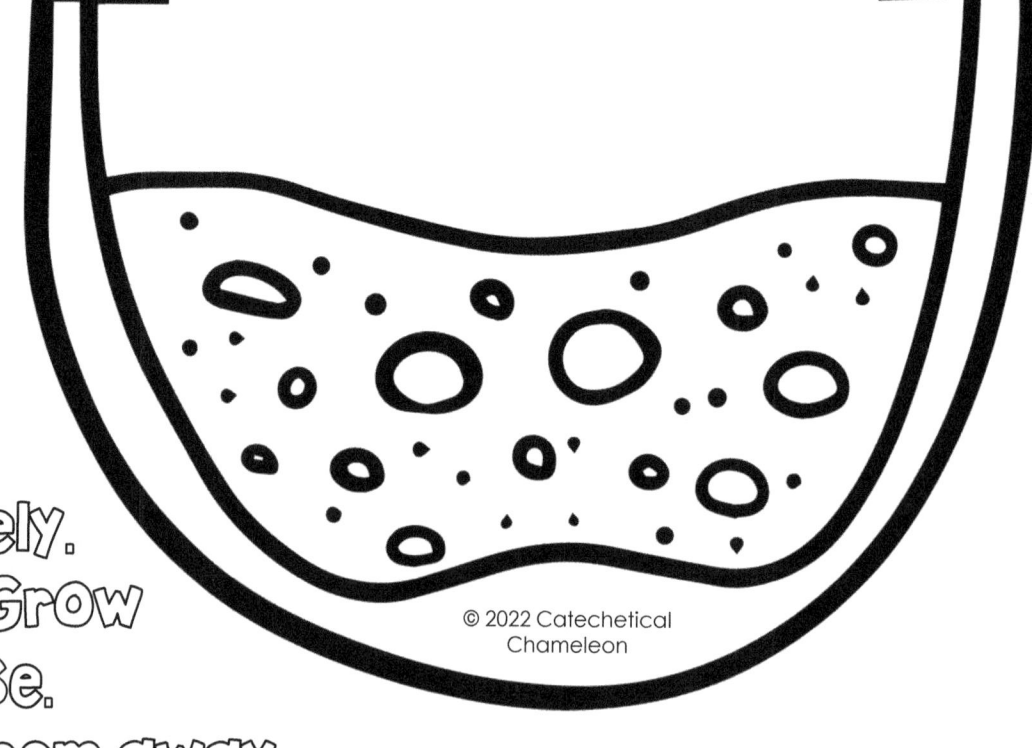

© 2022 Catechetical Chameleon

When we see others in need, we should think of it as if we see Jesus in need, because people in need are his loved ones. List the Corporal Works of Mercy that were mentioned in this Gospel below.

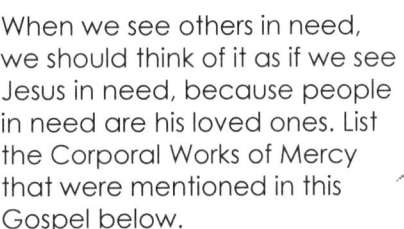

Our God is one who would wear a crown of thorns and die for us, but he is also a God who must judge us and sort the good from the bad. What an incredible kind of king! Write inside the sheep and goat what each represents.

Choose a quote about the glory of Jesus as king of the universe from this Gospel and write it inside the crown.

Our Lord Jesus Christ, King of the Universe

Matthew 25:31-46

© 2022 Catechetical Chameleon

LENT

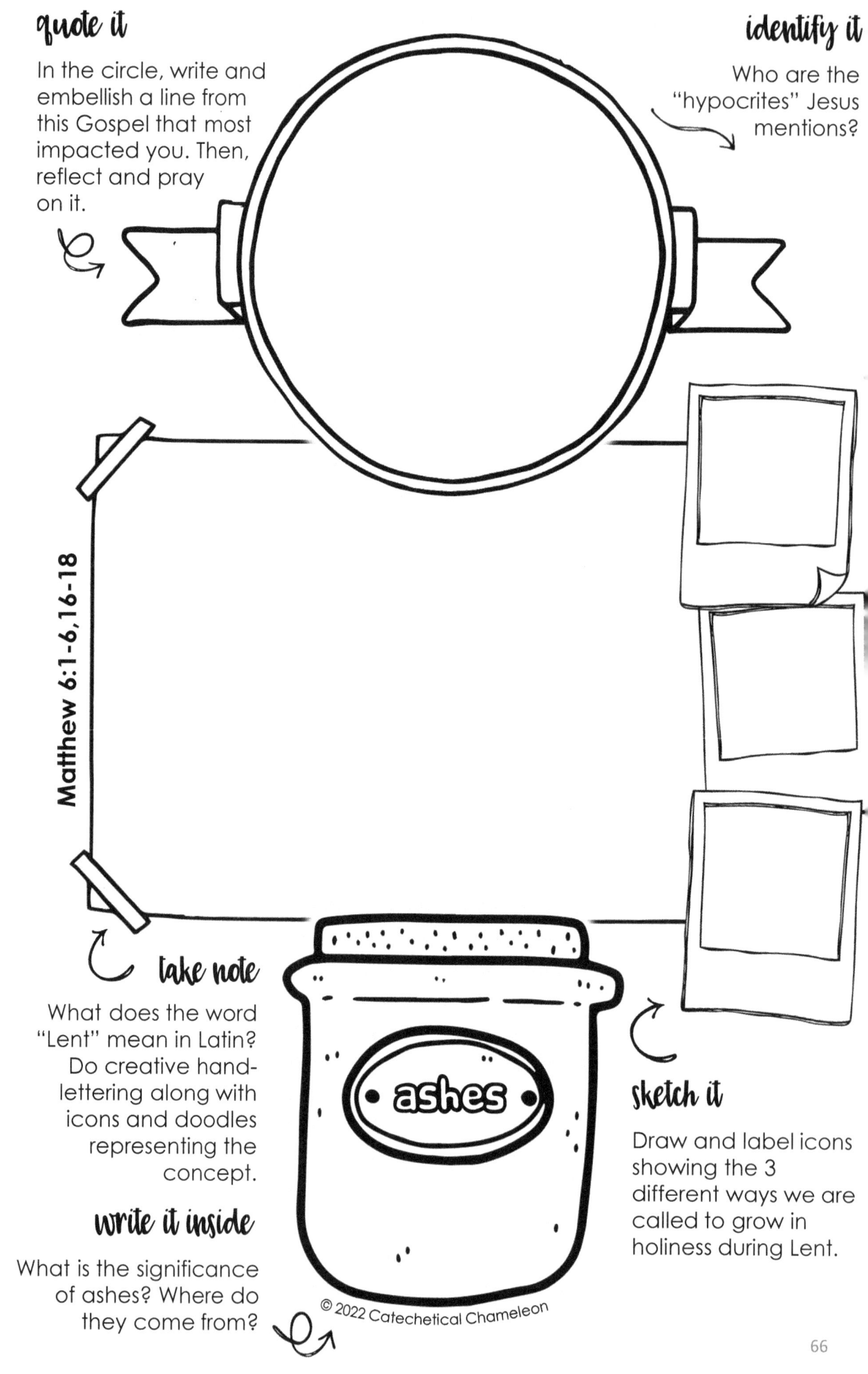

Your Father Who Sees You Will Repay You

quote it
In the circle, write and embellish a line from this Gospel that most impacted you. Then, reflect and pray on it.

identify it
Who are the "hypocrites" Jesus mentions?

Matthew 6:1-6, 16-18

take note
What does the word "Lent" mean in Latin? Do creative hand-lettering along with icons and doodles representing the concept.

write it inside
What is the significance of ashes? Where do they come from?

sketch it
Draw and label icons showing the 3 different ways we are called to grow in holiness during Lent.

ashes

© 2022 Catechetical Chameleon

66

Get Away, Satan!

In the top 3 circles, sketch images of the three different ways that Satan tempted Jesus.

Matthew 4:1-11

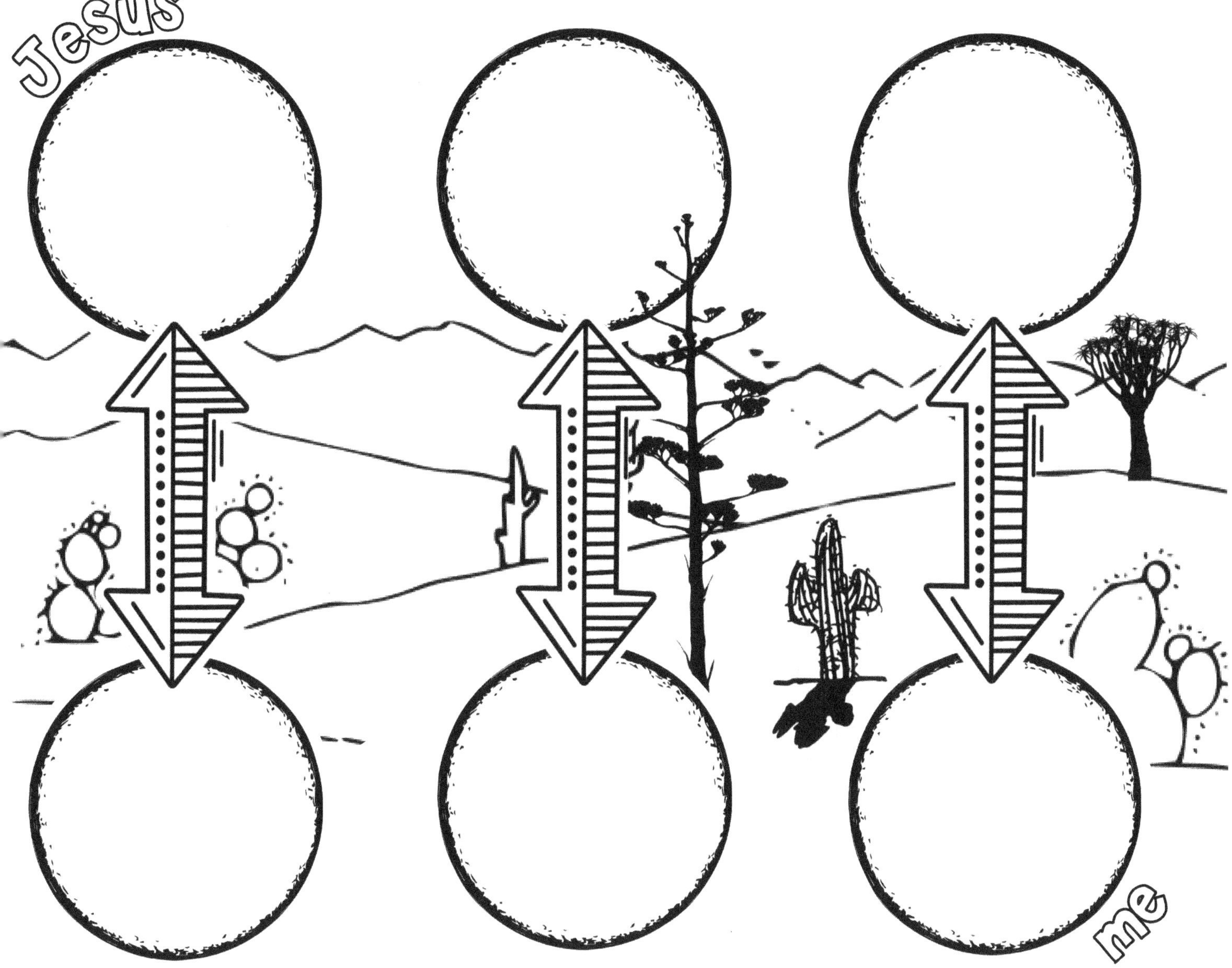

Jesus

me

What are the top temptations that you are battling right now? If you call them by name here, then pray for strength to resist them, you will be more likely to remember to call on Jesus in the moment that they next appear. Notice them and turn to God, who can always help you resist Satan. Identify your own main 3 temptations (in either words or images) in the circles below each of the ways that Jesus was tempted.

What does the "desert" represent for us? What are the times in human life that we may be figuratively in the desert?

© 2022 Catechetical Chameleon

The Man Born Blind
John 9:1-41

Side A

Side B

Why did the Pharisees disagree? What were they split about? Write some example statements that people nearby may have heard from each side as they debated.

Answer each inside the eyes to the right:
1. In what way was the man blind?
2. In what way were the Pharisees blind?
3. In what way(s) are *you* ever blind?
4. In what way(s) are people of today's world sometimes blind?

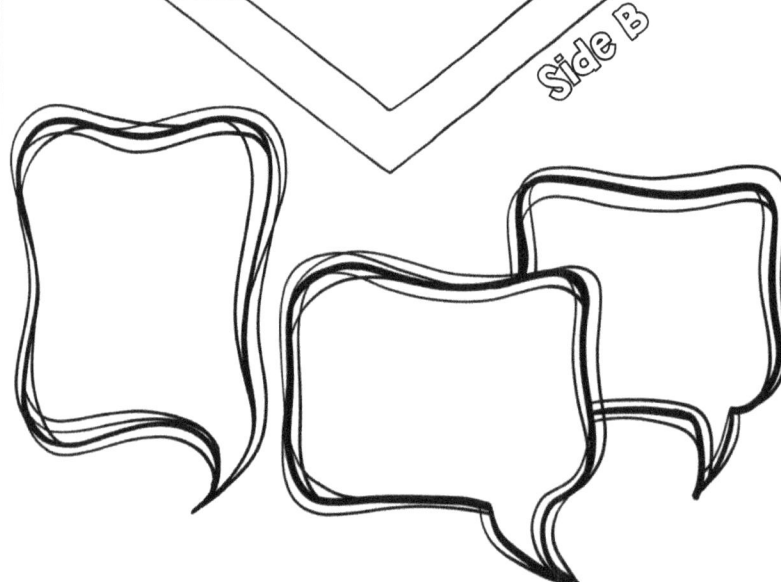

The Raising of Lazarus

In the two arrows, compare the resurrection of Lazarus to the resurrection of Jesus. List as many similarities as you can.

Lazarus / **Jesus**

Jesus wept

What do Jesus's tears tell us about Him?

Write a prayer around the border of the page, or within the rays of the rising sun in which you talk with God about the concept of resurrection and eternal life.

"I am the resurrection and the _____; whoever believes in me, even if he dies, will _____, and everyone who lives and believes in me will _____."

John 11:1-45

© 2022 Catechetical Chameleon

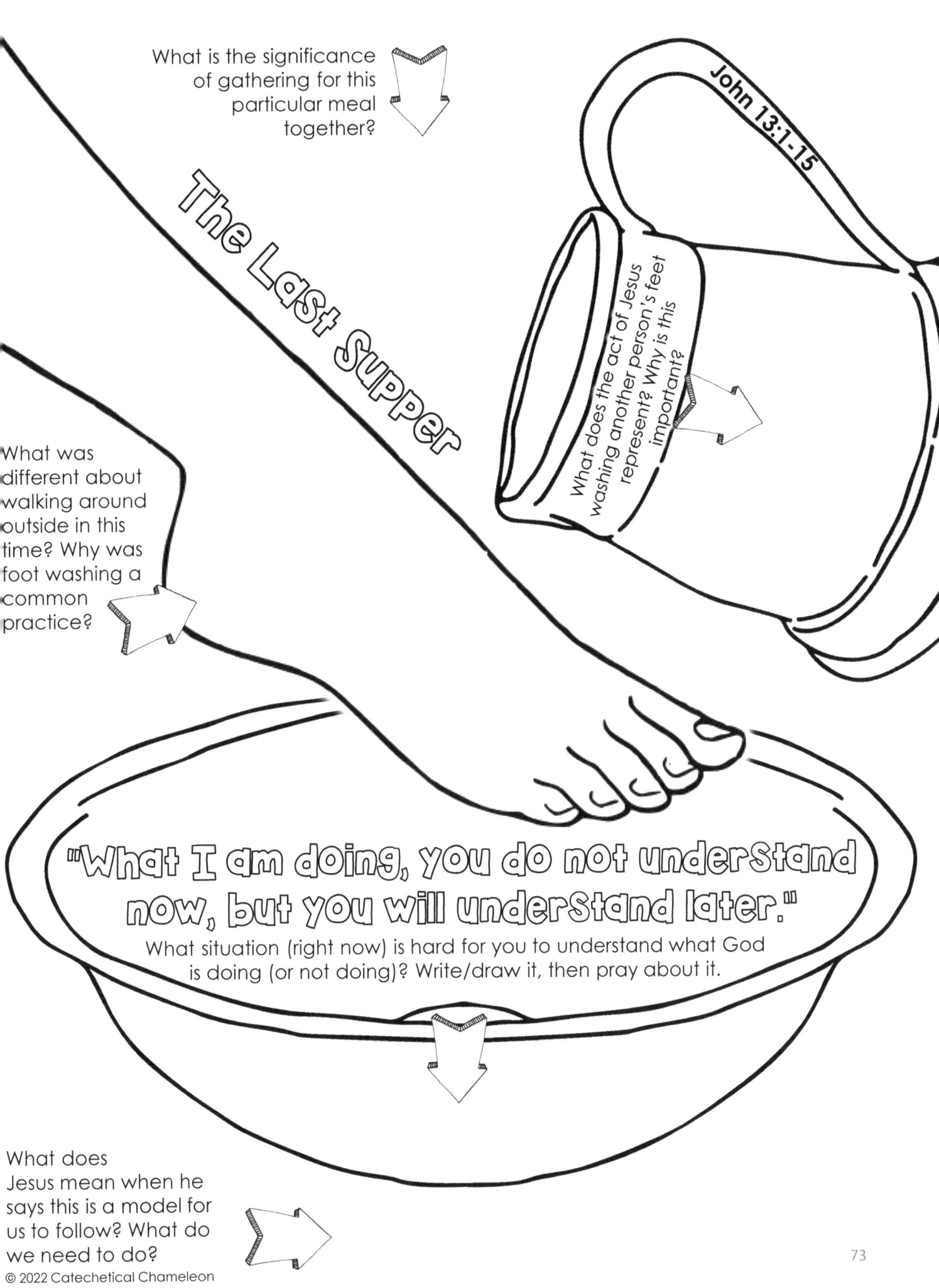

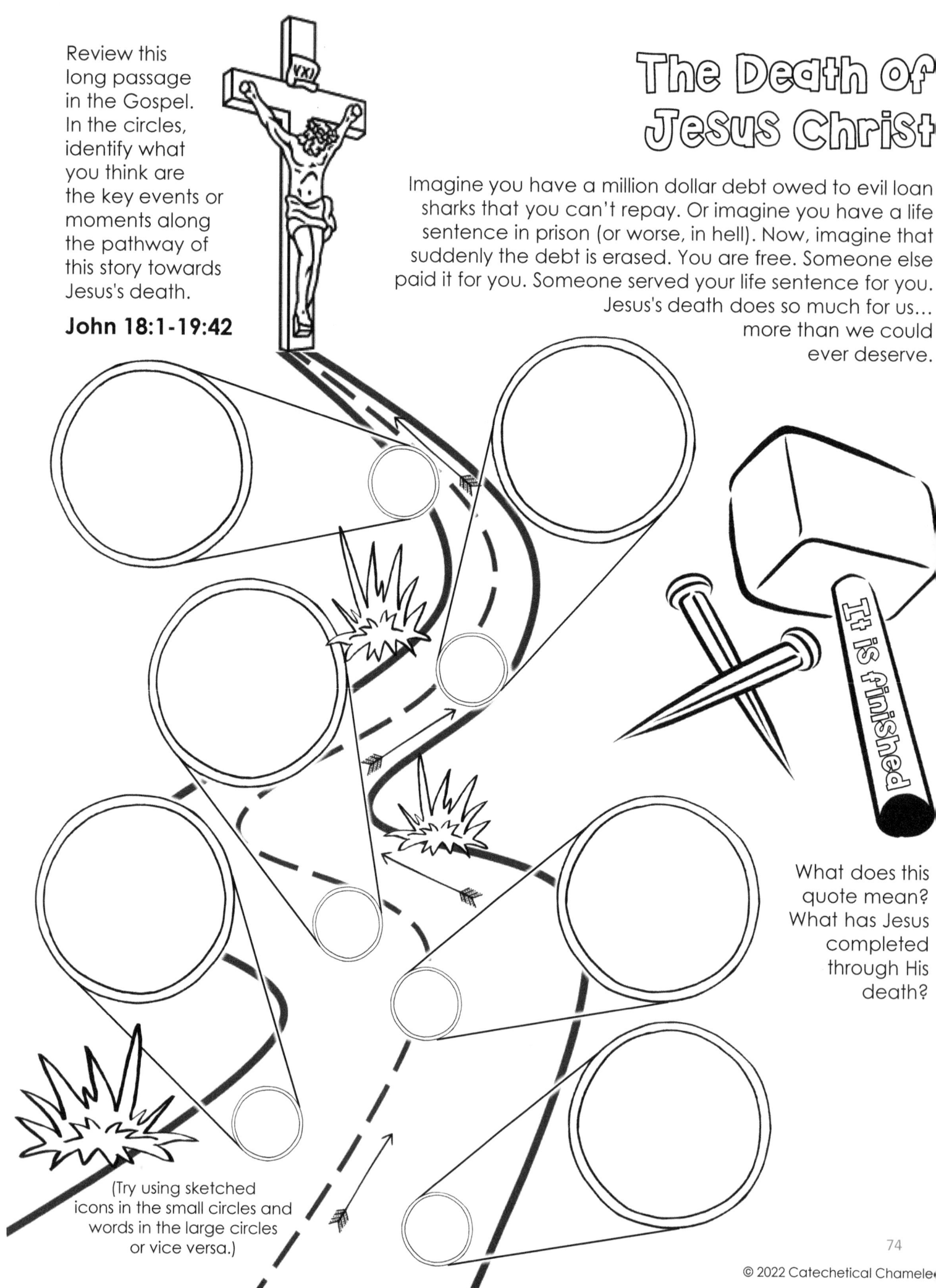

EASTER

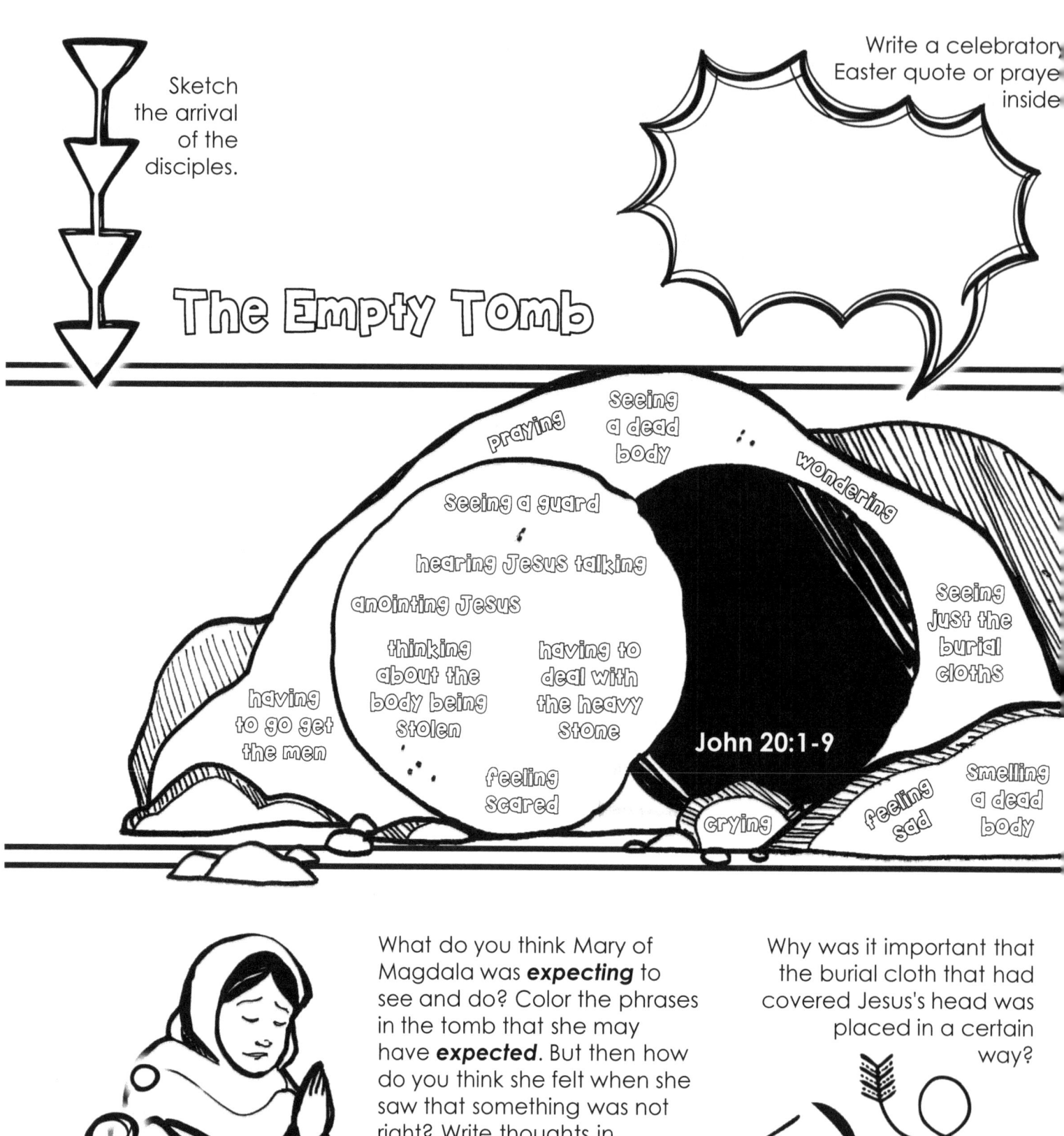

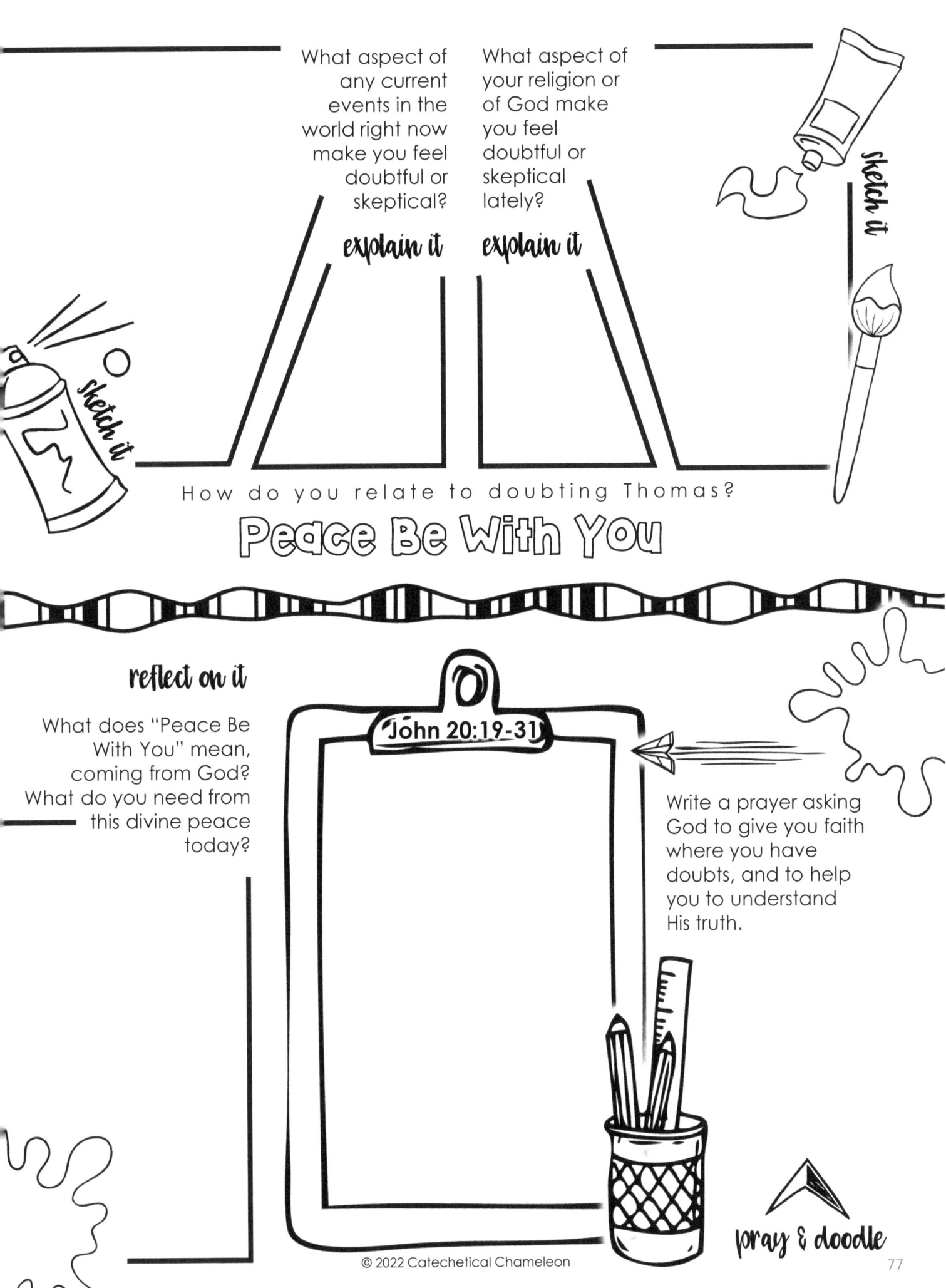

The Road to Emmaus
Luke 24:13-35

Draw the 2 disciples on the path walking away in defeat and include speech/thought bubbles showing what they were likely saying and thinking.

Draw yourself on the path walking away from something in your own life in defeat. Include a speech and/or thought bubble.

Like these two disciples, we sometimes are blind to the truth of the Resurrection and of Christ's victory, because the problems of the world can feel defeating or overwhelming. Draw icons that represent those problems or this feeling for you lately.

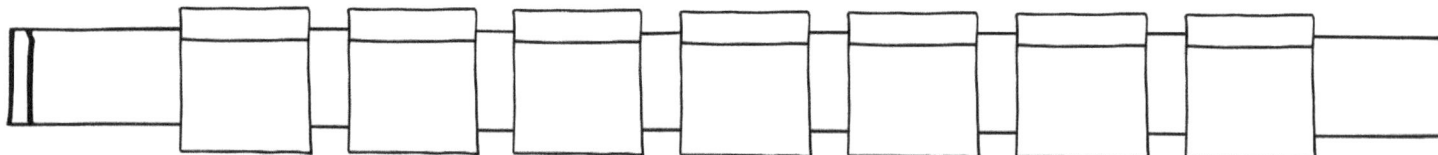

How did Jesus turn their thoughts back around and show them the hope? He had won, not been defeated! What did they learn?

How does Jesus help you to turn back toward hope? Reflect, and write and say a prayer for help when you feel defeated.

to do(odle) list:

- ❑ Inside the gate, explain what it means for Jesus to be the gate.
- ❑ Above the gate, create a sign labeling where this gate leads us. What are we entering "through" Him?
- ❑ Around and over the fenceposts, write who would try to sneak in the wrong way (both in the literal examples from this Gospel, and also who you think this would refer to now).
- ❑ In the background, within the blank space above (that represents the area behind the gate), use embellished lettering and/or sketches to depict Jesus's promise that we "might have life and have it more abundantly."
- ❑ Color, reflect, and pray.

I am the Gate

John 10:1-10

The Way, Truth, and Life
John 14:1-12

Color code the many quotes from Jesus (right column) in this Gospel to match up with the meaning / significance of each of his statements (left column). Use your best judgement to pair each with one or more of these truths based on what you think it means.

 God the Father and Jesus are united as one God.

 Jesus is now with God the Father in heaven.

 We can get to heaven too, and there is a place ready for each of us there.

 We can only get to heaven and be with God if we follow, know, and love Jesus.

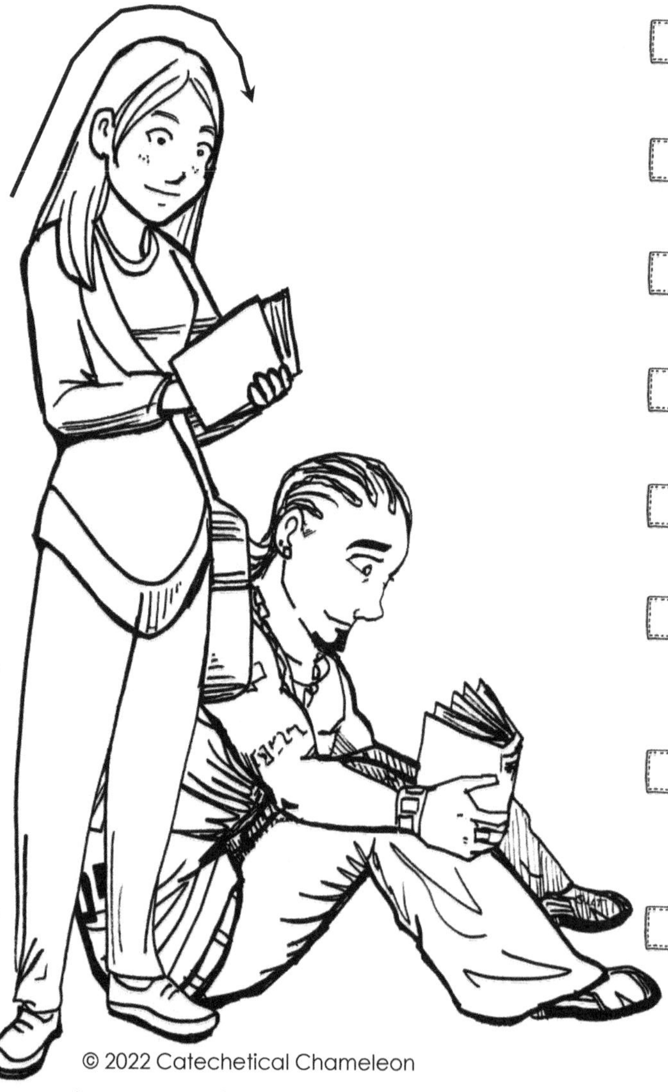

- "You have faith in God; have faith also in me."
- "In my Father's house there are many dwelling places."
- "I am going to prepare a place for you."
- "If I go and prepare a place for you, I will come back again and take you to myself, so that where I am you also may be."
- "Where I am going you know the way."
- "I am the way and the truth and the life."
- "No one comes to the Father except through me."
- "If you know me, then you will also know my Father."
- "Whoever has seen me has seen the Father."
- "The words that I speak to you I do not speak on my own. The Father who dwells in me is doing his works."
- "Believe me that I am in the Father and the Father is in me, or else, believe because of the works themselves."
- "Whoever believes in me will do the works that I do, and will do greater ones than these, because I am going to the Father."

Sum up what "the way, the truth, and the life" means:

The Spirit of Truth

John 14:15-21

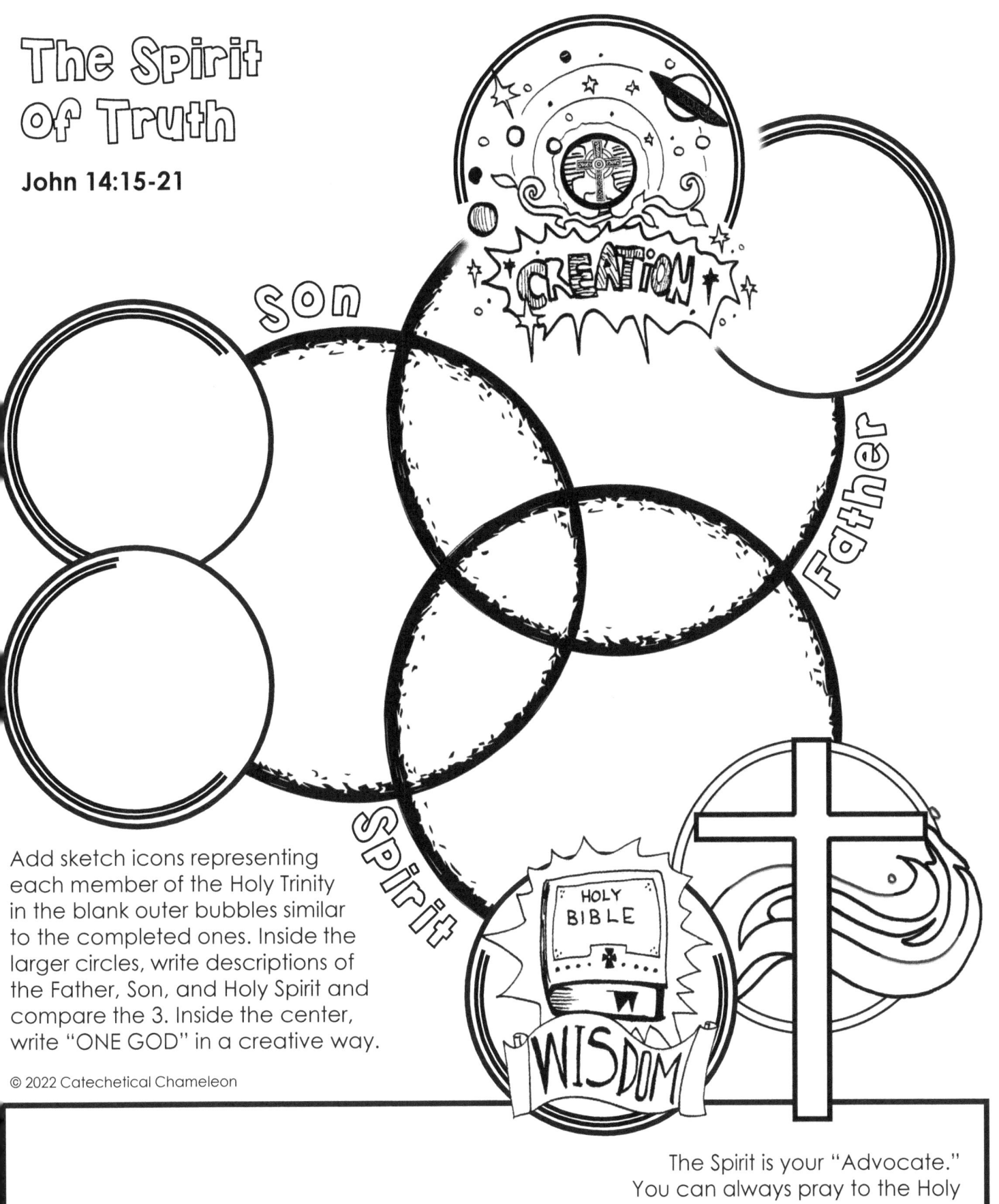

Add sketch icons representing each member of the Holy Trinity in the blank outer bubbles similar to the completed ones. Inside the larger circles, write descriptions of the Father, Son, and Holy Spirit and compare the 3. Inside the center, write "ONE GOD" in a creative way.

© 2022 Catechetical Chameleon

The Spirit is your "Advocate." You can always pray to the Holy Spirit when you need support in your life. Write a prayer here that you can use to pray for guidance, strong decision making, or consolation.

The Hour Has Come

John 17:1-11

This Gospel is very important. It tells us so much about Jesus, God's plan for Him, and His feelings about us. What truths are revealed to the disciples who overheard this prayer of Jesus speaking to His Father in heaven?

Inside the stopwatch, write your own prayer similar to this prayer Jesus prays to His Father. Pray about when YOUR hour of death approaches.

Reflect on what changes you may need to make to better glorify God. What work does God have for you? Pray about this question, then sketch representations of two areas of focus that you specifically need to grow in / work on to glorify God.

Go Make Disciples of All Nations

"Go, therefore, and make disciples of all nations, _____ them in the name of the Father, and of the Son, and of the Holy Spirit, teaching them to _____ all that I have _____ you."

"Behold, I am with you _____, until _____."

What does it mean to be a disciple?

disciples

How does God call each of us to use our different talents and personalities to spread the Good News of Jesus in a variety of different ways? Pretend you are the author of a story about how these 4 teens spread God's word. Give each of them 3 talents and/or personality traits, and write those on their clothing. Then, in the bubbles above, tell how each of these different people can be a disciple in their own way based on who they each are. Then, color!

HOLY DAYS

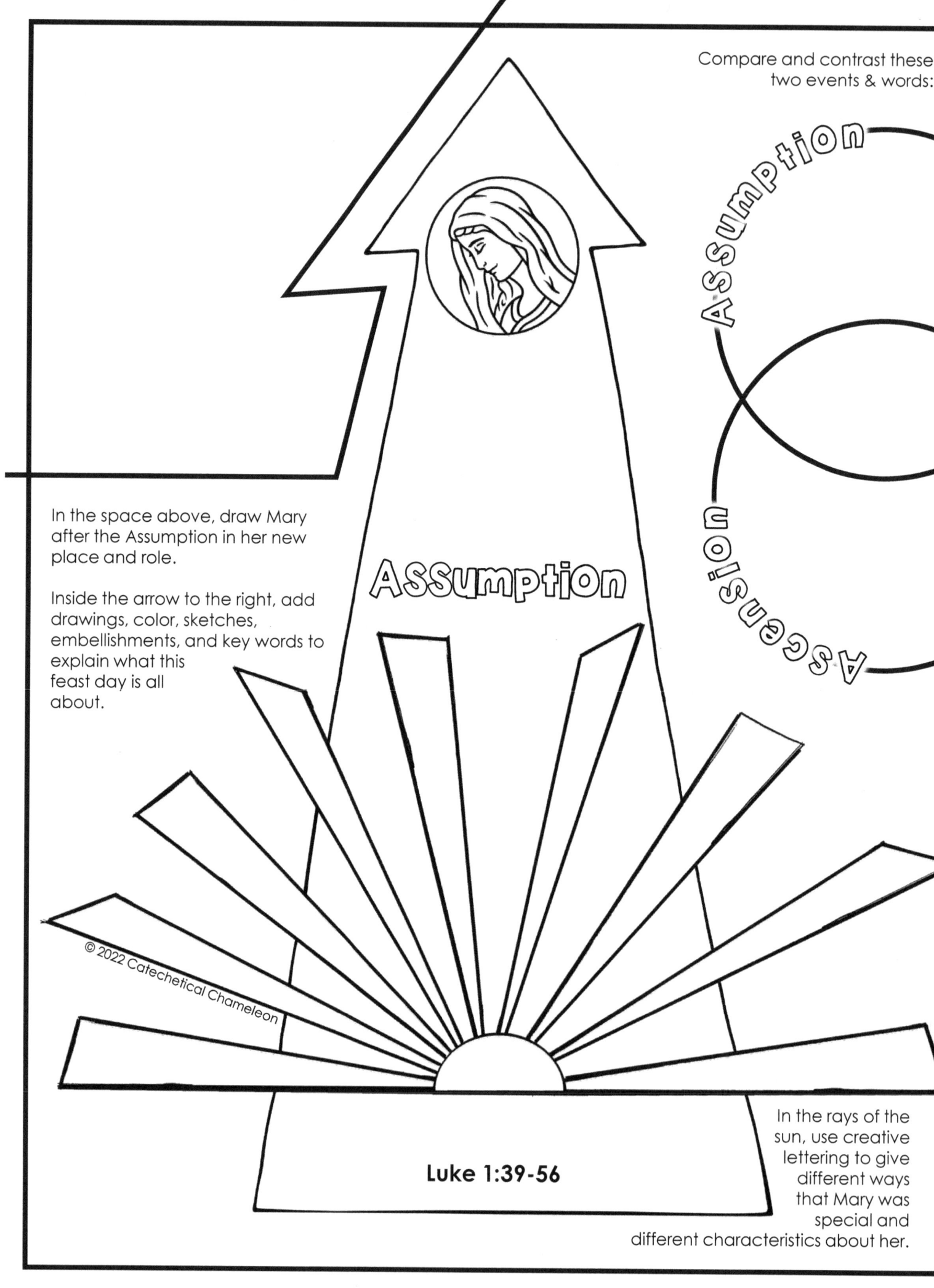

BONUS PAGES

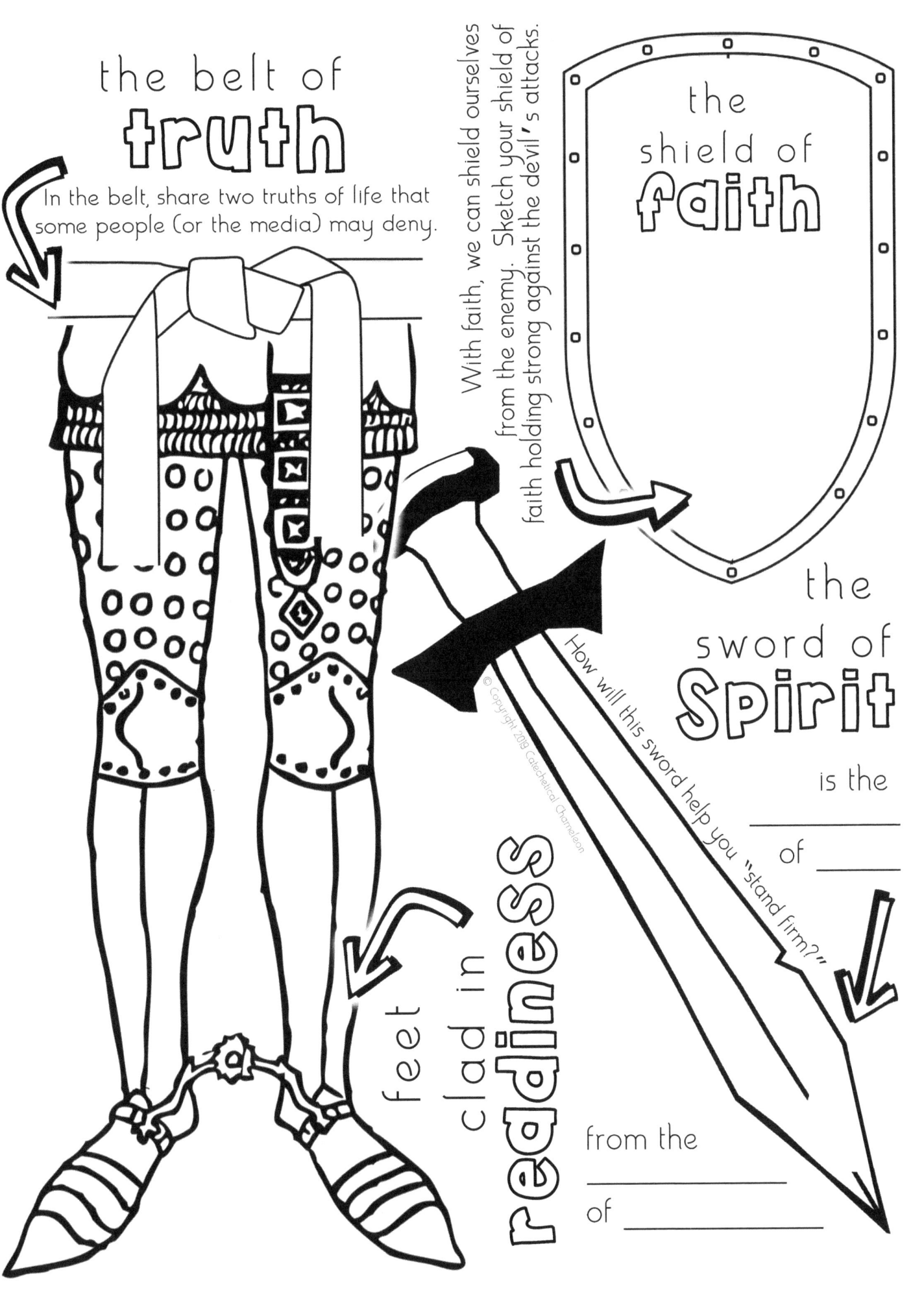

- ☐ Color the words around the perimeter of the calendar using the color listed.
- ☐ Fill in the blanks to show what each color represents.
- ☐ Write the season of the church year inside each sector.
- ☐ Show the seasons of the regular calendar year outside of the circle.

Name: _____

The Liturgical Calendar

SUNDAY GOSPELS
CYCLE YEAR "A"

INTRO TO THE GOSPELS

The Gospels

Background information: The word "Gospel" is from the Greek for "good tidings" or "good news." The Gospels tell the story of Jesus's life, ministry, and death. These historical documents offer 4 different perspectives of the events. They were written by men named Matthew, Mark, Luke, and John.

Timeline: Jesus was born between 6 BC and 4 BC, and began his ministry and teaching when he was around 30 years old. His death was between 30 and 36 AD. Almost 40 years after that (probably sometime around approximately 70AD), Mark wrote his account of Jesus's life. Matthew's account was written sometime between 75 and 90 AD. Luke wrote his between 80 and 95, AD, and John wrote his after 95 AD.

Help students reflect: Why is it important that we have 4 different accounts of the same historical events? What is the point of reading the Gospel? Why do we still study these texts thousands of years later?

The 4 Evangelists

Background information: The 4 different Gospel writers each wrote for a slightly different audience, and had a different perspective. We honor these men as saints.

Summary: Matthew was Jewish (like Jesus) but was greatly disliked by the Jewish people because he worked as a tax collector for the Roman government. Jesus passed by his tax collection booth and called him to "follow" Him, and Matthew did! He is often represented with an image / icon of an angel. Matthew's audience was primarily those who were already Jewish.

Mark met Jesus when he was a young boy. He writes a fast-paced, exciting account of the events that occurred. It's a short Gospel compared to the others. His symbol is a lion. He spoke to the Romans, with emphasis on action and power.

Luke's gospel is long and detailed. It focuses more than the others on Mary and the Nativity and also on Jesus healing people. Luke is represented by an ox. His audience included the Greeks, who focused on culture, beauty, and truth.

John was a young apostle, and his Gospel is more poetic. It is written more in a mystical, heavenly way, and is sometimes more symbolic. His symbol is an eagle because his Gospel is less "grounded" and soars above the earthly things. John's Gospel was written for *everyone*!

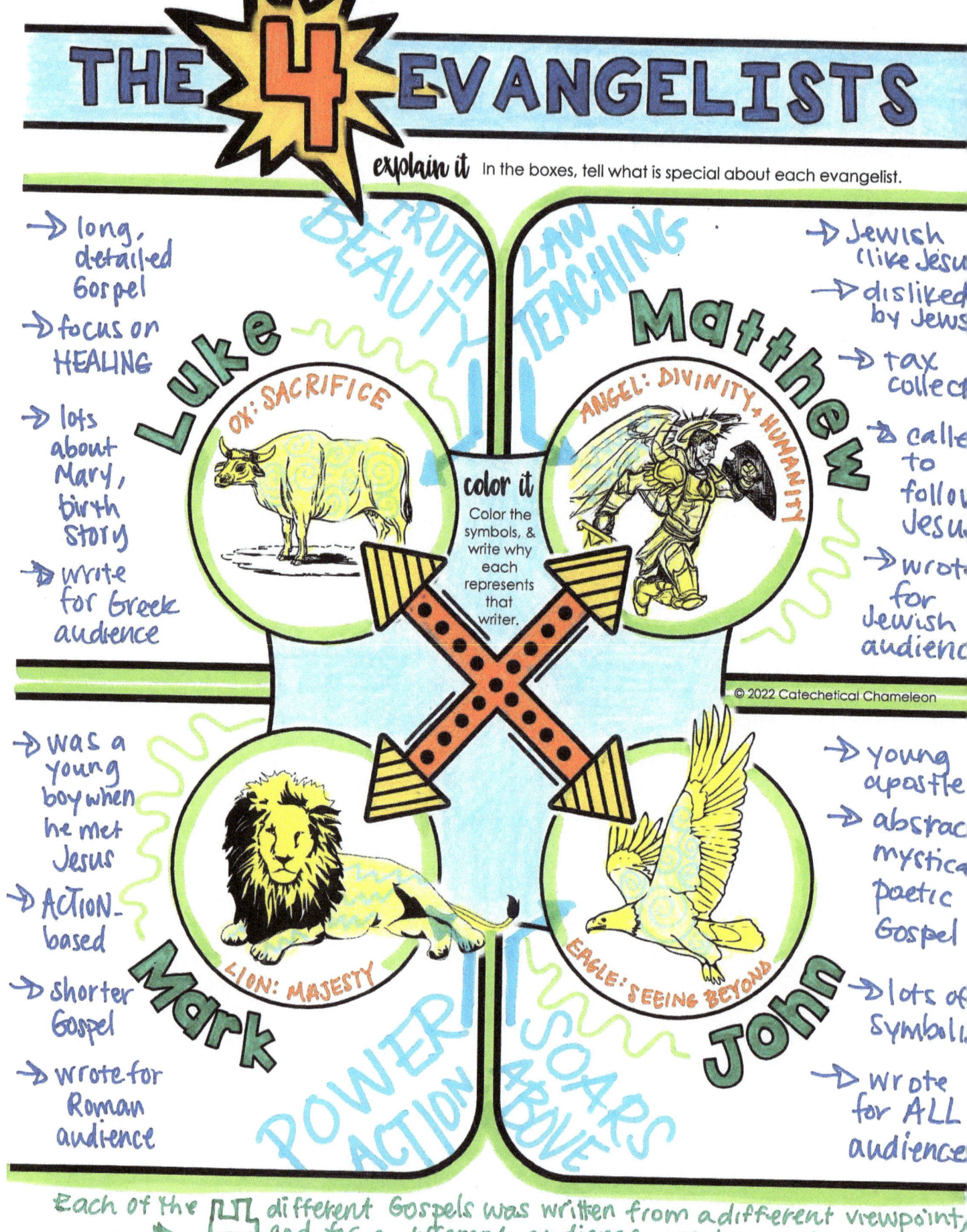

Teacher Notes: Gospel Doodle Reflections   Cycle Year "A"

Scripture Citations

Background information: The Bible is a collection of many books. The Old Testament includes stories from before Jesus was born. The New Testament includes accounts of Jesus's life and beyond.

Citing Scripture: To find a passage to read, you first find the book within the Bible (in the example shown, we would find the Gospel of Luke. Then, within that book, you can reference the chapter and verses to read the correct section. The book and chapter number come before the colon, and the number of the line to start reading comes right after the colon. If there's more than one verse to read, the ending verse will be listed too. Occasionally, a passage crosses into another chapter. You may have a citation that lists one chapter and verse, then continues through another chapter and verse. Just remember that the colon placement is always (chapter): (verse(s)).

Help students reflect: What special prayer is being introduced in the beginning of Chapter 11 of Luke's Gospel? Isn't it so incredible that this prayer that we still use today comes straight from Jesus's own teaching?
In John's Gospel, Chapters 18 and 19 are the account of how Jesus died. We would probably be most likely to hear this part during Holy Week.
Take a few moments on your own to flip through the Bible. Can you find a passage somewhere in the Bible that feels relevant to you today? How would you cite the line(s) if you wanted to remember where to find them to read again, or if you wanted to share them with a friend?

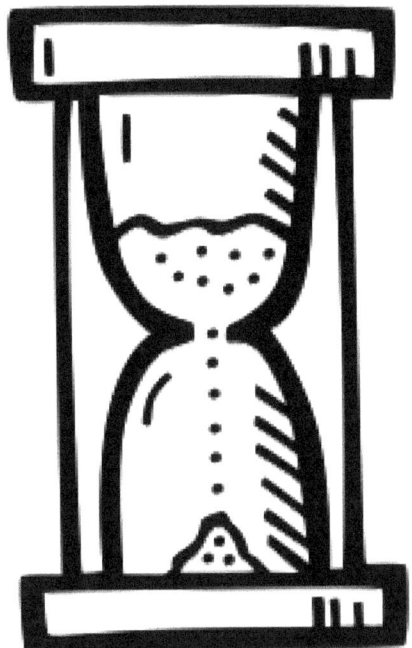

ADVENT

Teacher Notes: Gospel Doodle Reflections   Cycle Year "A"

The Day and The Hour are Unknown

ADVENT

1st Sunday of Advent
Matthew 24:37-44

Background information:
- The "Parousia" is a Greek word for arrival and signifies the arrival of Jesus at the end of time.
- The "Son of Man" is an expression that refers to Jesus. (Jesus speaks of himself in the third person here.)

Summary: In this parable, Jesus announces that he will return to build His kingdom of peace and joy, without pain on Earth. There will be no more suffering! The separation of people one from another shows that we cannot judge who is ready to receive Jesus and who is not. We can only prepare our own hearts!

Help students reflect: This parable can be frightening! Jesus's return means that people will be separated from each other. But Jesus does not mean to make us afraid. He means to show us how urgent it is that we look inside at our own hearts and see whether we have room for Jesus in our lives. Would we be ready if Jesus came in a few months? What about a few minutes?

John the Baptist Preaches

2nd Sunday of Advent
Matthew 3:1-12

Background information:
- The Kingdom of Heaven is the kingdom Jesus will return to establish.
- Pharisees and Sadducees were the clergy of Jesus's day.

Summary: St. John the Baptist tells us we need to repent to prepare ourselves for Jesus's coming. He says this especially to the "religious" people who act and seem like they are pursuing holiness, but whose hearts are far from God. John also tells us the "method" for cleaning our hearts which is to remember our Baptism when we were washed with the fire of God's love for us.

Help students reflect:
In what ways might God be calling me to "prepare the way of the Lord?" How can I bring Jesus into the world?
I don't want to be someone who looks 'religious' but whose heart really isn't into Jesus... Are there any ways I need to repent?
What are some of the good fruits I've produced? Did I help a friend through something difficult? Did I clean something up without being asked? Maybe I spent quality time with someone without complaining...?

a kingdom of PEACE & JOY is coming

The Day and the Hour...

Jesus will come again! Use creative lettering to write the Greek word for his "ARRIVAL" within the airplane.

PAROUSIA...

Matthew 24:37-44

PREPARE for the ARRIVAL

are Unknown

Identify a frightening thought that this Gospel may bring into your mind.

Identify a peaceful / joyful thought that this Gospel may bring into your mind.

sketch it — Who is the "Son of Man?"

It's JESUS!

SON OF MAN

We do not know when! Am I ready for Jesus?

reflect on it

How will you prepare? Write a short prayer below.

pray about it

Lord, Please prepare my heart and mind for your coming. Let me always be **ready** for you and for your ARRIVAL. AMEN.

Peace Joy no Pain no suffering

Draw some icons that represent what Jesus' kingdom will be like. What will be there, and what will exist no longer?

prepare your heart

we do not know the hour.

© 2022 Catechetical Chameleon

Teacher Notes: Gospel Doodle Reflections   **Cycle Year "A"**

What Did You Go Out to See?

ADVENT

3rd Sunday of Advent
Matthew 11:2-11

Background information: As Jesus begins his preaching ministry, John the Baptist is taken into prison by King Herod of Jerusalem. From prison, John is doubting whether or not Jesus is the real deal, the messiah for which Israel has been waiting for hundreds of years. Is Jesus the one who will lead God's chosen people to freedom?

Summary: Jesus rebukes John the Baptist for doubting that Jesus is the messiah. Nonetheless, Jesus then goes on to tell that John the Baptist is the greatest of the prophets who foretold the coming of the messiah because John alone "prepared the way of the Lord." Jesus also reminds the people gathered that despite John's location/appearance/way of life, there was something that attracted the people to John.

Help students reflect: Sometimes we can doubt whether or not Jesus is really there to help us. Can I remember any times that Jesus helped me or my family out of a tight spot? What was that like? The Church can sometimes today look unattractive or seem burdensome. When have I liked being a part of the Church? What did I like about it? What was that feeling like?

Mary & Joseph

4th Sunday of Advent
Matthew 1:18-24

Background information:
- Mary & Joseph were engaged (not yet married) when Mary was found pregnant.
- In the Old Testament, God often speaks through angels.
- In the Old Testament, there were other examples of divinely influenced pregnancies with which Joseph would have been familiar.
- The name given to Jesus means "Yahweh (God) saves."

Summary: God gave Mary a miracle baby that put her in a very difficult spot with Joseph. Joseph had to assume that Mary was an adulterer, and adulterers were stoned to death by the Jewish police. Joseph and Mary both knew this, but Joseph was such a good guy and loved Mary. He decided to quietly end the marriage instead. But God spoke to Joseph and helped Joseph understand the divine plan happening through their marriage. The marriage was saved, and Mary and Joseph prepared to bring the baby Jesus, who is God, into the world.

Help students reflect:
How would you react if an angel spoke to you in a dream and said that God gave you/your wife a miracle baby and the baby was going to save the whole world?
With faith as strong and powerful as Joseph's, what would you trust God to do in your life?

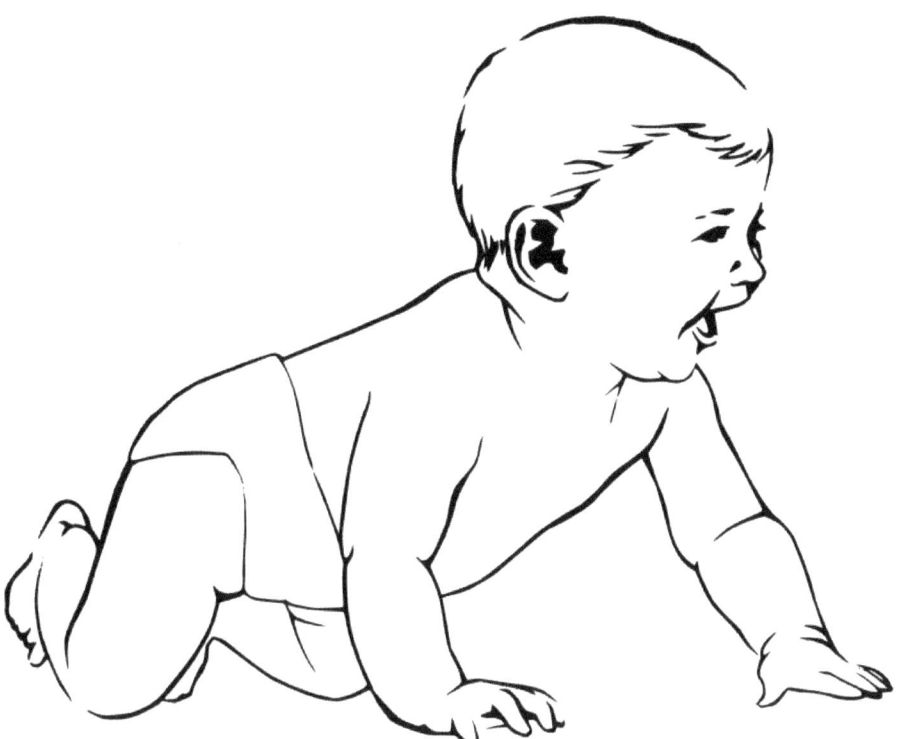

CHRISTMAS

Teacher Notes: Gospel Doodle Reflections **Cycle Year "A"**

The Genealogy of Jesus

Christmas Vigil
Matthew 1:1-25

Background information:
• The Old Testament predicted that the Messiah would be born of Abraham's lineage. Some doubted Jesus's lineage and therefore his claim to be 'Messiah,' so Matthew was concerned with establishing Jesus's claim to Abraham.
• Matthew's lineage includes the names of four women—Tamar, Rahab, Ruth, and Bathsheba—who had strange/unexpected pregnancies in order to make Mary's virgin pregnancy more comfortable to his reader.

Summary: Mary's pregnancy while engaged to Joseph made her seem an adulterer. Joseph, a merciful and then strong man, sought to quietly protect Mary through divorce but then with strength of faith trusted God's messenger to see the marriage through. Jesus's birth is penetrated with God's supernatural providence and natural tragedies in marriage.

Help students reflect: What makes babies wonderful? What makes them annoying? Do I believe that the all-powerful God became a helpless baby? If I do, what does that mean to me? And if I had faith like Joseph and Mary, what would I trust God to do in my life?

The Word Became Flesh

Christmas Day
John 1:1-18

Background information:
• St. John writes using a lot of themes from the philosophy of his day. Therefore, this is a favorite passage of many theologians.
• In ancient philosophy, the "Word" was the reason and logic of the universe. John here identifies Jesus as the rationale prior even to the universe, ordering all for good.
• "A man named John" refers to John the Baptist, the forerunner of Jesus.
• "The Word became flesh." Here, John dramatizes Jesus's birth as God who is behind and before the entire world taking on a human body and life, with all of its weakness.

Summary: St. John the evangelist writes some confusing verses here. But he does so to highlight in many ways how the unlimited, all-powerful, perfect, all-good God of light descended into a limited, weak, broken, and difficult dark world of human life. God did this to save us. The great God became small to show us how close He is to us. God became a baby and died on a cross so that we can believe, no matter what, that He loves us.

Help students reflect:
Does the light shine in the darkness? When life is hard, what are some "lights" that you can remember? What is it like to be a child of God? Would you think of God as your Father? What are some graces or some truths that you want from God? Do you believe that God would give you those? Has He already given you those?

Teacher Notes: Gospel Doodle Reflections   Cycle Year "A"

Running from Herod

The Holy Family of Jesus, Mary, and Joseph
Matthew 2:13-15, 19-23

Background information:
- King Herod was the ruler of Jewish people appointed by Roman Marc Antony. He was extremely anxious about the possibility of insurrection and heard that a rival "King of the Jews" had been born in Bethlehem. Herod murdered all of the infant males in the town in what became known as the "Slaughter of the Innocents." Jesus and his family escaped.
- The first King Herod ruled during the time of Jesus's birth. He was likely assassinated by his son Archelaus who succeeded him to the throne. A second King Herod, Herod Antipas, took over soon after and is the Herod who executed John the Baptist.

Summary: In a dream, Joseph is warned by an angel of King Herod's plot for murder. He is told to flee, and escapes to Egypt with his family. When the danger has passed, Joseph receives word that it is safe to return.

Help students reflect: Even Jesus, who is God, was protected and guarded by his family. In what ways have your mother and/or father protected you? What does a mother or father's protection look like? Do you think God has protected you through your parents?

The Visit of the Magi

The Epiphany of the Lord
Matthew 2:1-12

Background information:
- The Magi are the wisemen of Jesus's day. These particular Magi are astrologers.
- The Magi understood the prophecy placed on Jesus, that he is the King of the Jews.
- Gold, frankincense, myrrh were gifts appropriate to royalty in Jesus's time.
- Because the Magi did not tell Herod where Jesus was, Herod plans to murder every child in the region in the "Slaughter of the Innocents."

Summary: King Herod conspires to use the Magi to find Jesus, whom Herod wishes to murder to save his own kingship. The Magi understand Herod's duplicity, and do not tell Herod where Jesus is. Instead, they honor Jesus with kingly gifts and leave Herod to his wrath.

Help students reflect:
If your country had a king, would you honor him? Would you trust him to protect your land and family and livelihood? Do you see Jesus as your King? If so, what kind of gifts would you want to give him?

The wise men found Jesus by gazing up at the sky. When you look at the sky, what do you find? How does it make you feel? Do you ever find Jesus that way?

ORDINARY TIME

Teacher Notes: Gospel Doodle Reflections Cycle Year "A"

The Heavens were Opened

The Baptism of Jesus
Matthew 3:13-17

Background information:
- The Baptism of the Lord is the moment Jesus is made ready for ministry and called the "Son of God."
- The phrase "to fulfill all righteousness" means the salvation of mankind. It does not mean that Jesus was himself sinful, but it means that Jesus is identifying himself with sinners.
- That the heavens were opened means that there is a new relationship between God and human beings. This newness is caused by Jesus's identification with sinners.

Summary: Jesus travels from Galilee to his cousin John at the Jordan River. John recognizes that he needs Jesus's baptism and is surprised that Jesus asks for John's baptism. Jesus humbles himself and is baptized. God reveals himself in the Holy Spirit. He reveals who Jesus is.

Help students reflect: Jesus's baptism is like our baptism. The Holy Spirit comes upon us, and God speaks the truth that destroys our sinfulness: that we are His beloved children. Do you know on what day you were baptized? If not, ask your parents. That is your Christian birthday! Remember that God does not judge or condemn you, only loves you as His son/daughter. What does this mean to you? What does it mean that Jesus identifies with our weaknesses?

John's Testimony to Jesus

The Second Sunday of Ordinary Time
John 1:29-34

Background information:
- "Lamb of God" refers to the conquering lamb-who-was-slain, the paschal lamb which saved Israel in the Exodus, or the servant of God led like a lamb to slaughter as an offering for sin (in the prophet Isaiah). John's Baptism was all about revealing Jesus to Israel.
- Key quotes: "Behold, the Lamb of God, who takes away the sin of the world," "He is the one who will baptize with the Holy Spirit," "He is the Son of God."
- The dove was a symbol of God's new creation (after the Flood in the Noah story).

Summary: After John the Baptist baptizes Jesus, he continues to preach in order to make people aware that Jesus is around, and that Jesus is the Son of God. He has seen and testifies that the Holy Spirit came down upon Jesus and that Jesus baptizes with the Holy Spirit.

Help students reflect: John the Baptist has waited for this moment for his entire life. He knew the Messiah would come and now Jesus has. Even more, the Messiah showed John the Holy Spirit and the Father, and the Messiah is the Son of God. You can imagine John's excitement. In life, we will not always be as excited as John to share Jesus, but have we been that excited some of the time? Has there been a time when you were so struck by the amazing gift of God's love for you that you had to share it? Do you believe in this kind of love that God has for you? If you do, what makes it hard to share it sometimes? How can we get better at talking about God's love?

Teacher Notes: Gospel Doodle Reflections **Cycle Year "A"**

Beginning Ministry in Galilee

The Third Sunday of Ordinary Time
Matthew 4:12-23

Background information:
- John was arrested by King Herod Antipas (the nephew of the King Herod of the infancy narratives) and eventually beheaded. His fate foreshadows the death of Jesus under the same Herod.
- The prophecy for Naphtali and Zebulun matters because they were the first Israelite lands to be ransacked by the Assyrian conquest of 733BC. Now, Jesus shows them favor.
- For Rabbis to have disciples was ordinary in this time. But disciples were made out of the educated 1%, who had spent ten years in school, passed multiple exams, and personally sought out Rabbis to follow. Jesus flips this upside down by calling the uneducated.

Summary: After the death of John, Jesus begins his public ministry in Galilee by proclaiming the Kingdom of God. Jesus calls Simon and Andrew from their nets. Then Jesus calls John and James away from their fisherman-father, Zebedee. The first disciples are made.

Help students reflect: Why do we have to repent at the arrival of the Kingdom of Heaven? Why do you think Simon, Andrew, James, and John all were able to leave their way of life so easily? What is it about following Jesus that can seem too good to be true?

The Beatitudes

The Fourth Sunday of Ordinary Time
Matthew 5:1-12a

Background information:
- The poor in spirit (Hebrew: anawim) are those who are materially poor, but also who have a deep trust in God. It means a beggar.
- The word "heaven" originally was a Jewish word that just meant "God." Only later did the word come to mean "a place" the way we use it today.
- Purity of heart means that your goodness extends down to the depths of who you are.
- Shalom is the Jewish word for "peace." Shalom is the fullness of God's gifts.
- Matthew's beatitudes are 8 in number, while Luke's are 4 (Luke 6:20-23).

Summary: Going up the mountain so the crowd could hear, Jesus begins his Sermon on the Mount with eight beatitudes: Blessed are: the poor, mourners, the meek, the righteous, the merciful, the pure, the peacemakers, those who are persecuted for righteousness, and the insulted on account of Jesus. Have students pull out Bibles to reference the full text of the beatitudes.

Help students reflect: Which beatitude most strikes a chord with you? Why? Which beatitude does our world struggle with the most today? Which beatitude is the world the best at these days? What do the beatitudes say about the way God loves us? What do the beatitudes say about the way we ought to treat other people?

ORDINARY TIME

Beatitudes

Which one of these does the world need to re-think and adjust right now?

▶ poor in spirit

Which one of these do you need to personally reflect on?

▶ persecuted for the sake of righteousness

© 2022 Catechetical Chameleon

In the balloon: RICHES & glory on earth ≠ riches/glory in God's eyes or in heaven. We must become humble and prioritize what God values, and we'll be REWARDED in heaven

from the Sermon on the Mount

Beatitudes
Matthew 5:1-12a

In the balloon, sum up the big idea behind what Jesus is teaching in this sermon. To the right, complete each of the beatitudes.

Color code it: Color the beatitudes that you find most tricky/complicated in one color that you identify here: 🔴 and the ones that seem obvious / easy to you in another color that you identify here: 🟢

Blessed are they who mourn	for they will be COMFORTED
Blessed are the poor in spirit	for theirs is the KINGDOM of heaven
Blessed are the merciful	for they will be shown MERCY
Blessed are they who are persecuted for the sake of righteousness	for theirs is the KINGDOM of heaven
Blessed are the meek	for they will INHERIT the land
Blessed are the peacemakers	for they will be called CHILDREN of GOD
Blessed are they who hunger and thirst for righteousness	for they will be satisfied
Blessed are the clean of heart	for they will see GOD

Teacher Notes: Gospel Doodle Reflections   Cycle Year "A"

Salt and Light

The Fifth Sunday of Ordinary Time
Matthew 5:13-16

Background information:
This week continues with a passage from Jesus's Sermon on the Mount.

Summary: Jesus gives us a simple message that our actions matter, and they are seen. If we lose our good works, what good is it to call ourselves Christians? Rather, because we call ourselves Christians, we ought to take care to do good in the world, so that our good deeds shine, and those who see them can glorify God.

Help students reflect: How are you doing as a Christian? Does your life look like Jesus's life to other people? Where in the last week have you been salt for another person's day (seasoning, flavor, the spice of life!)? Where in the last week have you been like salt that lost its taste? How do you relate to being called "a city set on a hill?" Do you relate to being called "the light of the world?"

Amen, I Say to You

The Sixth Sunday of Ordinary Time
Matthew 5:17-37

Background information:
- These various teachings continue Jesus's Sermon on the Mount.
- Jesus is modifying or rejecting the Mosaic, Jewish Law. He does this not to abolish it, but to fulfill God's promise of a new way of life for all of humanity.
- Moses had permitted divorce in the Old Law. Jesus changes this with an exception for marriages between family members.
- Gehenna is another word for hell.

Summary: In these new teachings, Jesus is affirming the real challenge and difficulty of the kind of life he is laying out. To enter Heaven, to live the way Jesus lives, our righteousness has to surpass even that of the Pharisees (the priests of the day!). Jesus tells us he is not abolishing what Moses wrote down, but is fulfilling God's promise of blessing to Moses. It's a promise we can share if we amend our lives.

Help students reflect: Does Christianity seem like too many rules? Have you experienced that Jesus gives us rules to protect us and help us to thrive?
How do we go about making sure we are reconciled with our brothers/sisters? How do we control our bodies and keep them from sin? Why is Jesus so serious about us keeping our promises? Why is honesty so important?

ORDINARY TIME

Teacher Notes: Gospel Doodle Reflections　　　　　　　　　　　　　　　　　Cycle Year "A"

Love Your Enemies

The Seventh Sunday of Ordinary Time
Matthew 5:38-48

Background information:
- This passage is a part of the Sermon on the Mount.
- Moses's Law actually did allow for retaliation (Leviticus 24:20).
- The Roman soldiers that occupied Palestine were allowed to demand property or services from the native peoples.
- Jesus expands the Old Law about loving neighbors. Now, "neighbor" includes the people who are actively seeking our ruin.

Summary: Jesus gives two new provisions about the way we should treat our aggressors. We don't retaliate against people. We love our enemies.

Help students reflect: These are two of Jesus's most difficult teachings in the book. Love your enemies and turn the other cheek. Who do you know that is really good at loving people, even people who may not always treat them well? Can you think of anyone who has exceptional patience and is able to turn the other cheek? Think of some ways these rules about treating others could change your school and home. What would be an advantage of practicing these rules in the next phase of your life?

Don't Worry About Tomorrow

The Eighth Sunday of Ordinary Time
Matthew 6:24-34

Background information:
- This passage is a part of Jesus's Sermon on the Mount.
- "Mammon" is a word that means "wealth," or "property." It is more general than "money."
- "Life-span" could also be translated "stature" as in "height." Jesus is talking not only about lengthening our lives, but growing our own sense of importance.

Summary: Jesus tells us unequivocally that we must choose to serve either God or the world. Serving the world ties us down to many cares and worries that can ruin our happiness. Living for God, on the other hand, frees us to live as the children of a loving Father who takes care of all of our needs.

Help students reflect:
Practice this meditation: close your eyes and take a moment to reflect on some of your needs, cares, worries. When you are imagining these things say, "My heavenly Father knows that I need them all." Something like this can be a way for us to practice trusting in God. Why do you think Jesus says to "seek first the Kingdom and righteousness?" How does that help me fix the things that worry me?

"Leave it with me. Just RELAX and go to sleep. I've got your back and will always be here."

Jesus is waiting patiently for your attention. He wants to be with you. What do you think He is saying to you if you pray and really listen?

HIGH school applications

my MOM'S HEALTH

online gaming with FRIENDS

But seek FIRST the kingdom of GOD and his righteousness and ALL these things will be GIVEN you besides

What are the top 3 things that you give your attention to, worry about, or focus on instead of putting them in Jesus' hands and then turning your eyes to Him? Sketch those worries and distractions above.

Matthew 6:24-34

© 2022 Catechetical Chameleon

Don't Worry About Tomorrow

Color, Relax, Reflect, and Pray!
As you focus on this image, pray about your own worries, then make a commitment to Jesus to choose God over material things and the distractions of the world.

Teacher Notes: Gospel Doodle Reflections — Cycle Year "A"

True Discipleship

The Ninth Sunday of Ordinary Time
Matthew 7:21-27

Background information:
- The Sermon on the Mount begins in the 5th Chapter of Matthew. Jesus goes up a mountain with his disciples and he begins to teach. Chapters 5, 6, and 7 of Matthew's Gospel recount the teachings of Jesus on a variety of topics including Beatitudes, anger, loving your enemy, dependence on God, and the path to Heaven.
- The Sermon on the Mount gives the disciples a clearer understanding of what makes someone a true follower of Christ. By this time in His Sermon, Christ is addressing the promise of heaven, and the importance of building life on solid foundations.

Summary: After giving the Beatitudes and many other teachings, Jesus provides the Disciples with more clarity on how to be a true disciple and receive the reward of heaven. He teaches that not everyone who desires Heaven will have it, even if they claim to act in Christ's name. Only those who truly do the will of God will enter the Kingdom of Heaven.

Help students reflect: What is easier: saying you want to get to heaven, or following God's will? How do you know if you're following God's will? Why do you think people have a hard time following what Jesus said in this Gospel? How can you build your life on solid ground?

Jesus Calls

The Tenth Sunday of Ordinary Time
Matthew 9:9-13

Background information:
- In the time of Jesus, tax collectors had a bad reputation. It was common for a tax collector to charge people more than they actually owed, and then keep the extra money for themselves.
- The Pharisees, who were very strict about Jewish Laws, considered Tax Collectors to be ritually unclean, because they worked with pagan (Roman) coins. So tax collectors had a reputation of being impure.

Summary: Jesus calls Matthew, a tax collector, "Follow Me." This parallels the calling of the first disciples, and Matthew responds as they did by following Jesus. Jesus shares a meal with many tax collectors and sinners, and the Pharisees are scandalized by Jesus and question why Jesus would do this. Jesus replies, "Those who are well do not need a physician, but the sick do."

Help students reflect:
Are there people that you don't want to associate with because of their reputation? What do you think Jesus would do in that situation? In what ways do you need Jesus's healing?

Teacher Notes: Gospel Doodle Reflections　　　　　　　　　　　　　　　**Cycle Year "A"**

Mission of the Apostles

The Eleventh Sunday of Ordinary Time
Matthew 9:36-10:8

Background information:
- The Twelve Apostles: Jesus chose twelve in order to draw a connection to the twelve tribes of Israel which composed the original Kingdom and honor the Israelite people. They are apostles because they are sent: apostle means "sent one."
- Jesus shares His ministry with the apostles: healing, driving out bad spirits, proclaiming the Kingdom of God, and even raising the dead.

Summary: After the disciples have journeyed with Jesus, witnessing His miracles, and being taught by Him for some time, Jesus sends them out as His apostles to begin performing His ministry. It is game day for the disciples. How will they do?

Help students reflect: The apostles were the first evangelists for Jesus. Their job was to heal people, raise up good spirits, and proclaim the Kingdom by curing the sick, raising the dead, cleansing lepers, and driving out demons. Where in your life have you experienced healing? Where do you need it now? (Remember that sometimes healing can be painful.) Who has healed you? Who raises your spirits? Who proclaims to you the Kingdom of God? Do you heal people, or raise their spirits, or proclaim the Kingdom? If you don't right now, notice that the disciples didn't do it right away either. First, they had to learn how and had to grow strong enough. What do you need to be ready to heal, encourage, and proclaim?

Do Not Be Afraid

The Twelfth Sunday of Ordinary Time
Matthew 10:26-33

Background information:
- Last week, Jesus prepared to send his twelve apostles out into ministry. This week, he continues that preparation by encouraging the apostles not to be afraid.
- Healing people, encouraging, and proclaiming the Gospel causes social stress. People tried to attack Jesus multiple times for the healings He performed and the message He preached. That is why Jesus had to encourage the apostles before He sent them out to do the same.

Summary: Jesus continues His preparation of the twelve apostles for public ministry. He tells them not to be afraid, that there is no secret that can remain forever, and that the Father is taking care of them always. Finally, Jesus tells them that He will tell the Father about them if they are faithful to Him.

Help students reflect:
Why were people so upset with Jesus for doing good things for people? Can you think of any examples today where Jesus gets people upset? Does Jesus ever upset you? Where and why? This would be a great thing to talk to a priest about. If you acknowledge Jesus, have you experienced the peace and fearlessness He gives? What is that experience like?

Teacher Notes: Gospel Doodle Reflections Cycle Year "A"

Conditions of Discipleship

The Thirteenth Sunday of Ordinary Time
Matthew 10:37-42

Background information:
This reading is the conclusion of the theme of the last couple of weeks in which Jesus gives the pros of discipleship and the cons of unfaithfulness.

Summary: When we choose anything wholeheartedly there are all-encompassing consequences. In choosing Jesus, we choose to love Him even more than our own parents, more than our own life. And when we live this way, we truly become Jesus to others, because His life lives inside of our own. The people who care for you, because you are Jesus's disciples, have cared for Jesus Himself.

Help students reflect: Have I made a firm commitment to follow Jesus? Have I chosen Jesus with my whole heart or have I tried to negotiate living for Jesus according to some limit or percentage: only certain parts of His teachings, or only sixty percent? How have I taken up my cross in my life in order to follow after Him? Have I been able to experience what great joy this brings Jesus? How have I given "a cup of cold water" to the people who bring Jesus to me? How might I try to do that this week?

Come to Me

The Fourteenth Sunday of Ordinary Time
Matthew 11:25-30

Background information:
- The "wise and learned" refers to the Scribes and Pharisees. Though they have learned much and hold a high place in society, they have rejected Jesus's teachings and miracles.
- Revelation comes from the Father as a free gift to those who are willing to accept it as children. The arrogant are those who do not receive as a little child and cannot receive the Father's revelation. Revelation comes from the Father through the Son (Jesus), who chooses those to whom He will reveal it.

Summary: Jesus takes a break from his teachings on unfaithfulness in this Gospel to praise the Father, explain His relationship to the Father, and to teach us how we are to share in this relationship: joining Jesus's yoke and labor, being like little children.

Help students reflect: Does Jesus's yoke seem easy? Does His burden seem light? Have you heard Jesus's invitation to have rest in your own life? What does that look like? What is the lighter burden and the easier yoke that Jesus is inviting you to? What is the difference between being childlike and childish? Why does Jesus tell us to be childlike but not childish? Why can the Father only be revealed to us by Jesus?

ORDINARY TIME

Teacher Notes: Gospel Doodle Reflections　　　　　　　　　　**Cycle Year "A"**

Parable of the Sower

The Fifteenth Sunday of Ordinary Time
Matthew 13:1-23

Background information:
- This week is the start of a long series of Gospels in which Jesus teaches with parables. During this discourse, Jesus will offer several parables to illustrate for His listeners what He means by the "kingdom of heaven."
- PARABLE: a simple story used to illustrate a moral or spiritual lesson
- By using ideas and stories that are simple and relatable, He can reveal knowledge of the mysteries of the Kingdom of Heaven in a way that is easy to understand. There were many people who could not read or write. Jesus used memorable, simple stories to guide them to understand His teachings.

Summary: Jesus told a parable about a sower who was spreading seeds. Some of the seeds fell on the path, and birds came and ate them. Some seeds fell on rocky ground with little soil, and the seeds sprouted quickly, but they were scorched by the sun and died because they lacked good roots. Some of the seeds fell in with the thorn bushes and the thorns choked the seeds so they died, but some seeds fell on rich soil. The seeds that fell on good soil grew and produced abundant fruit. The disciples asked Jesus why He taught using parables, and he told them that He uses parables because it helps people actually listen and understand. Then Jesus explained that in this parable the seed sown on good soil is the one who hears the Word and understands it.

Help students reflect: When you hear the Word of God do you try to understand it? Will you nourish and help grow the seeds that God plants in you?

Parable of Wheat and Weeds

The Sixteenth Sunday of Ordinary Time
Matthew 13:24-43

Background information:
Jesus's audience would have know about growing and farming because this was one of the most common ways for people to earn a living and provide for themselves.

Summary: Jesus gives another parable to His listeners. He tells a story of a planter who plants good seed, but then an enemy sneaks into his field and plants weeds. When the weeds sprout the workers ask if they should tear them up, but the master replies "No, if you pull up the weeds you might uproot the wheat along with them." The master decides to let the weeds grow until harvest time, then he will order his workers to collect all the weeds to be burned and gather only the good wheat into the barns. He also tells a parable about a mustard seed, which is tiny, but grows into one of the largest plants.

Help students reflect: God wants us to be the good wheat that can be gathered into his barn. What is one way that we can grow and be healthy and holy wheat? Do you ever wonder why God allows bad people to keep living and cause harm? Think of them like the weeds. Also, remember the story of the great flood. Consider whether eliminating some evil could actually harm God's good people too.

ORDINARY TIME

Teacher Notes: Gospel Doodle Reflections *Cycle Year "A"*

Parables About the Kingdom

The Seventeenth Sunday of Ordinary Time
Matthew 13:44-52

Background information:
- Because of the civic chaos in Palestine at the time of Jesus, it was common for people to bury their valuables in the ground so that they would not be stolen.
- When Jesus speaks of the "new and the old," He is speaking of the teachings of the Old Testament (old) and of His own teachings (new).

Summary: The first two parables speak of the ultimate value of the Kingdom of God. The parable about the fish is similar to the parable about the wheat and the weeds in its emphasis on a last judgement between good and evil. Finally, Jesus teaches that the Old and New Testament belong together. They are both important and true and must be used together to get the full picture.

Help students reflect: What is the most valuable thing on this earth that I can imagine? Why would the Kingdom of God be worth more than that? What am I doing now to make sure that I will be counted among the good fish? Why do we need to hold the Old and the New Testaments together in order to know God? Why is the New Testament not enough?

Feeding the Five Thousand

The Eighteenth Sunday of Ordinary Time
Matthew 14:13-21

Background information:
- This story is the only miracle that gets told in each and every one of the four Gospels.
- This miracle story is meant to call to mind the Eucharistic feast that Christians celebrate now, the one that will be celebrated forever in Heaven, and also the historical feast of the "manna from Heaven" in Exodus Chapter 16.

Summary: At this point in Jesus's ministry, He has become so popular that thousands have begun following Him around the countryside seeking healings, a word of encouragement, or some wonderful sign to strengthen their faith. The crowd concerns His disciples, but Jesus recognizes the power of the moment and multiplies a handful of loaves and two fish so that the whole crowd of five thousand eats their fill.

Help students reflect: The disciples make a perfectly sane request to Jesus to send the crowd away. What do you think the disciples' reaction was to the miracle of everyone having enough to eat? How would you respond to Jesus after an event like this? How would you try to explain it to your friends and family if you were there and realized what had taken place? Where in the world do we need a miracle like this? Think about those who are hungry, but also those who hunger for peace or even emotional stability. This week pray to Jesus for a miracle of multiplication somewhere in the world.

Teacher Notes: Gospel Doodle Reflections   Cycle Year "A"

Jesus Walks On Water

The Nineteenth Sunday of Ordinary Time
Matthew 14:22-33

Background information:
- After big events, Jesus goes away by Himself to pray and decompress. In this Gospel, He goes away after the feeding of the five thousand.
- The "fourth watch of the night" means the early hours of morning, around 3am.

Summary: After the feeding of the five thousand, Jesus takes some time alone to pray. Meanwhile, the disciples' boat drifts out to sea fighting against the wind. In the middle of the night, while the disciples are struggling to control their boat, Jesus walks out to them on the waves and terrifies them all. Peter, gathering up his courage, steps towards Jesus until his faith falters and he sinks. Jesus rescues him immediately and asks Peter why he doubted. All the disciples are completely amazed and begin to recognize that Jesus is God.

Help students reflect: When have you experienced turbulent waves and a loss of control in your life? How did you get through it? Was faith a part of that journey? Would more faith have helped you to get through the storm? Remembering that the disciples just experienced the feeding of the five thousand, how do you think they feel now, just twelve hours later, when they witness Jesus walking on water? Why do you think Jesus showed them this? How do you think they talked about it after it happened?

The Canaanite Woman's Faith

The Twentieth Sunday of Ordinary Time
Matthew 15:21-28

Background information:
- The Canaanites were Gentiles, not Jews, and were not the main focus of Jesus's public ministry. That said, Gentiles understood that salvation could only come through the Jews.
- The word "dogs" is really translated from a word meaning "little dogs" or "puppies." Although this does not completely absolve the offensive language, it somewhat softens it.
- The healing of the Canaanite woman's daughter prefigures the acceptance of Gentiles into the church after Jesus's Resurrection.

Summary: As Jesus moves through the region of Tyre and Sidon (towns on the Mediterranean, north of the Dead Sea), a Canaanite (Gentile) woman approaches Jesus and asks for his ministry for her daughter. Jesus denies her because she is not a Jew, but she persists, showing her faith, and Jesus acquiesces. The daughter is healed.

Help students reflect: Can you think of any large groups or settings in which people tend to break into unhealthy "cliques?" How can we imitate Jesus's willingness to accept the Canaanite woman? How can we break down cliques? What healing do we need in our own lives? What healing do we need in our school?

Teacher Notes: Gospel Doodle Reflections Cycle Year "A"

ORDINARY TIME

You Are the Son of God

The Twenty-First Sunday of Ordinary Time
Matthew 16:13-20

Background information:
- Peter is unique among the apostles. This would develop into the "head and members" church structure with the 'pope' (successor to Peter) being the head of the bishops (successors to the apostles). Pope Francis has emphasized that this model is more collegial than hierarchical.
- The "church" Jesus founds on Peter is the community of Christians: Peter holds the important role of governance for the sake of unity.

Summary: Continuing the ministry north of the Sea of Galilee, Jesus asks His disciples to consider who exactly they think that Jesus is. Simon Peter speaks on behalf of the disciples that Jesus is the Son of God. Jesus recognizes that the Father gave this knowledge to Peter in a special way, and so He decides on that day that Peter would receive his new name ("Peter" means "rock"), that he would be a foundation of the church, and that Peter will have special authority.

Help students reflect: When you think of bishops and the pope what sorts of things come to mind? What does it mean that they are successors to the apostles? Why might it make sense that there would be one apostle leading the rest? Where do you see the church as a community?

Suffering Ahead

The Twenty-Second Sunday of Ordinary Time
Matthew 16:21-27

Background information:
- Jesus was able to predict the suffering he would endure because of His full knowledge of humanity. He understood that if He went back into Jerusalem, the religious leaders and people would try to kill Him (something which must have confused His disciples, especially when the crowds were singing His praises on the Palm Sunday entrance).
- Remember that the disciples expected the Messiah to re-establish the old Kingdom of Israel and drive the Roman soldiers out of their land.

Summary: As Jesus begins to move from north of the Sea of Galilee back south towards Jerusalem, He tries to prepare His disciples for what He knows is coming: a public death that will destroy His disciples' hopes for a political revolution. Jesus paints a stark picture of discipleship in this life but promises that the rewards of the Father's glory will be worth it!

Help students reflect: What do you understand and what confuses you about Jesus's prediction of His death? What do you understand and what confuses you about Jesus saying "take up your cross and follow me?"
What are some things that people your age might need to deny themselves in order to be disciples? What are some crosses that you may need to take up?

Teacher Notes: Gospel Doodle Reflections   Cycle Year "A"

I Am In the Midst of Them

The Twenty-Third Sunday of Ordinary Time
Matthew 18:15-20

Background information:
- Previously Jesus has been focused on how disciples are to act; now, Jesus teaches how to deal with disciples who sin.
- Observant, virtuous Jews did not associate with Gentiles or tax collectors.

Summary: Jesus gives a three-step process for dealing with Christians who are in the community, but sinning. He asks us to first offer a private rebuke. Then, if that doesn't work, we are to bring several witnesses. The last resort would be to bring the whole community. If they still do not listen to the whole church then they are no longer a part of it. In the last part of this Gospel, Jesus teaches us about His presence in our prayer.

Help students reflect: What is challenging about the model of correction Jesus proposes for us here? Have you seen this practiced successfully anywhere?
Why is it important that sin be kept out of our Christian communities as much as possible? What is it like for Jesus to be present in our prayer? When are some times that we have experienced His presence?

The Unforgiving Servant

The Twenty-Fourth Sunday of Ordinary Time
Matthew 18:21-35

Background information:
- Jesus's answer to Peter's question is not necessarily connected to the parable He tells.
- The debtor's promise to "pay back in full" is empty because of the size of his debt. The master forgives him out of pure mercy.
- The debt owed by the other servant is miniscule in comparison. The contrast serves to show how ridiculous it would be for a Christian, who has been forgiven everything by God in Heaven, to withhold forgiveness here on earth.

Summary: Peter asks Jesus a question about forgiveness which Jesus answers. Then, Jesus tells a parable about the way we must forgive others in light of how much God has forgiven each of us. Refusing to forgive others comes at an ultimate cost: sacrificing God's mercy to us in the final judgement and experiencing the suffering of a life without mercy.

Help students reflect: What is the hardest part about forgiving people? Who do you know that is really good at forgiving?
How do we receive forgiveness from the Father? How often should we ask for the Father's forgiveness? Why is the Sacrament of Confession the best way to receive the Father's mercy and forgiveness?

Teacher Notes: Gospel Doodle Reflections   Cycle Year "A"

The Father's Vineyard

ORDINARY TIME

The Twenty-Fifth Sunday of Ordinary Time
Matthew 20:1-16a

Background information:
This teaching was given at a time when Jesus had moved once again south from Galilee and into Judea, drawing closer to Jerusalem.

Summary: Jesus gives a parable to explain the Father's generosity to disciples. Laborers are hired for one day's work at nine o'clock, noon, three o'clock, and five o'clock. All receive the same daily wage. Those hired at nine o'clock receive a just wage and everyone else receives a generous wage. Those hired at nine o'clock are furious that they were not paid more given that they worked harder than the others. The parable is a warning to the disciples not to be jealous.

Help students reflect: Was any injustice actually done to those who worked the whole day? If not, why were they so upset? Was it really just envy?
When you were younger what kinds of things made you jealous? What kinds of things do older people get jealous about? How can we become people who are not jealous? What are some good strategies?

The Parable of the Two Sons

The Twenty-Sixth Sunday of Ordinary Time
Matthew 21:28-32

Background information:
• Tax collectors were basically Jewish traitors who worked for the Roman Empire to collect taxes from their fellow Jews (often collecting more than was necessary to pad their own pockets).
• Jesus tells this parable to the chief priests and elders: the sons symbolize the religious leaders and the religious outcasts. The outcasts end up doing God's will.

Summary: Jesus again chastises the religious elite of His day. He tells them this parable to show them that although they have said they will do the Father's will, in fact, they have not. And if that's not enough, the people the religious elite condemn (like tax collectors and prostitutes) are the ones that actually do end up doing the Father's will.

Help students reflect: Some people will look at us like we are religious leaders: we read the Gospel, we attend Mass, we pray, people know we are religious. How do we know that we are fulfilling the Father's will? How do we know that it is all more than show?
Why was Jesus so stern with the chief priests and elders of His day?
What are some strategies that we could work on to make sure that our religion is true? Is it better to give up religion entirely or to work to make sure that the religion I practice is real? Which option is more honest?

Teacher Notes: Gospel Doodle Reflections — Cycle Year "A"

The Tenants of the Vineyard

The Twenty-Seventh Sunday of Ordinary Time
Matthew 21:33-43

Background information:
- This parable is again directed to the Pharisees and religious leaders of the day. In a pretty dramatic way, Jesus condemns the leaders as evil men.
- "The Kingdom of God will be taken away and given to those who will produce its fruit" is a reference to the inclusion of the Gentiles in the future of the church.

Summary: Jesus tells a parable in order to explain who the Kingdom of God is for. The Kingdom is the vineyard and the landowner is God. The tenants are the Pharisees and the servants are the prophets who were routinely murdered by the religious elite in the Old Testament. The son is Jesus, of course, although the Pharisees possibly would have missed that detail. Jesus tells this parable in order to condemn the Pharisees for their corrupt leadership of the Jews and to justify the inclusion of the Gentiles in the church.

Help students reflect: Are we good tenants of the things we have been given? Do we take care of our clothing, our classrooms or surroundings, our possessions, and our chores?
Do we take care of strangers? Do we welcome strangers and make them feel at home? Do we produce the fruits of the Kingdom of God? What are some ways to produce peace, comfort, justice, charity, hope, and faith in our world this week?

The Parable of the Wedding Feast

The Twenty-Eighth Sunday of Ordinary Time
Matthew 22:1-14

Background information:
- The Kingdom of God is also depicted as a Wedding Feast in the book of Revelation.
- Some interpreters see the wedding garment as "the good deeds" that have to accompany a life of faith. The wedding garment might also symbolize the garment of baptism. It could also symbolize a willingness to be fully committed to the celebration, a lack of preparedness, or a wedding crasher who enters unjustly.

Summary: Jesus again tries to show what the Kingdom of God is by contrasting it with the tradition of murdering and mistreating God's servants. A king hosts a wedding feast, but twice his invitation is refused and the second time his messengers are murdered. The third time he collects anyone who will come but finds that there are some who come who are not worthy of staying. These ones are not chosen.

Help students reflect: For private reflection: Have I ever refused the invitation? Have I ever ignored the invitation? Has there been a time when I've sinned against the messenger? For conversation: How can we choose to accept the invitation now? Where is this invitation to join the Kingdom appearing in life? What does acceptance look like? Once we choose to accept Jesus's invitation, how do we make sure we are worthy of remaining at the feast?

Teacher Notes: Gospel Doodle Reflections　　　　　　　　　　　　　　　**Cycle Year "A"**

Repay to Caesar What is Caesar's

The Twenty-Ninth Sunday of Ordinary Time
Matthew 22:15-21

Background information:
- The Pharisees were a group of Jewish religious leaders who considered themselves more holy than others because they followed the Jewish Laws very strictly. They were opposed to the Roman occupation and rejected the idea of paying taxes to Rome.
- The Herodians were a group of Jewish people who supported Herod and collaborated with the Romans. They supported paying taxes to Rome.
- If Jesus agreed with the Pharisees he was an enemy of Rome, but if he agreed with the Herodians, then he wasn't following Jewish tradition.

Summary: The Pharisees and Herodians approached Jesus to trap him. They asked him, "Is it Lawful to pay the census tax to Caesar or not?" Jesus knew about their malice, so he took a Roman coin and asked whose face was on it. It was Caesar's. Then Christ said, "Repay to Caesar what belongs to Caesar, and to God what belongs to God."

Help students reflect: Do we get so wrapped up in the world around us that we forget to give God our attention and adoration? What is one thing that you can do this week to help you focus on God instead of on money and entertainment?

ORDINARY TIME

The Greatest Commandment

The Thirtieth Sunday of Ordinary Time
Matthew 22:34-40

Background information:
The Pharisees were again trying to test Jesus by asking him what the greatest commandment is. In the Mosaic Law, there were not only the 10 Commandments, but over 600 other laws and rules that also had be followed to live out the expression of the Jewish Covenant.

Summary: One of the Pharisees asked Jesus, "Teacher, which commandment in the law is Greatest?" Jesus responds, "You shall love the Lord your God with all your heart, with all your soul, and with all your mind. This is the greatest and first commandment. The second is like it: You shall love your neighbor as yourself." Jesus explains that the whole law and all the prophets depend on those two commandments.

Help students reflect: What is one way you love God with your whole heart? What is one way you love God with your whole soul? What is one way you love God with your whole mind? Describe one time when you loved your neighbor as yourself.

Teacher Notes: Gospel Doodle Reflections Cycle Year "A"

Whoever Humbles Himself

The Thirty-First Sunday of Ordinary Time
Matthew 23:1-12

Background information:
- There is growing tension between the Scribes & Pharisees and Jesus.
- The Scribes and Pharisees were hypocritical, and Jesus warns against using them as examples even though they do have authority.

Summary: Jesus told His disciples and the crowd to do and observe all of the proper Mosaic practices that the Scribes and Pharisees have decreed, but not to follow their example. Because of the legitimate authority of these Jewish leaders, Jesus reaffirms the importance of following what they say, but Jesus also points out that the Scribes and Pharisees "preach, but do not practice" and for this reason they are bad examples. Jesus comments that the Pharisees and Scribes do good works, so that they can be seen and they always try to increase their own importance, but the greatest must become a servant. Jesus says, "Whoever exalts himself will be humbled; but whoever humbles himself will be exalted."

Help students reflect: When have you tried to increase your importance or tried to be seen as better than you are, or better than others? When have you lessened your own importance to serve someone around you?

Parable of the 10 Virgins

The Thirty-Second Sunday of Ordinary Time
Matthew 25:1-13

Background information:
In Matthew's Gospel, Jesus has begun to prepare his disciples to receive the Kingdom of Heaven. Jesus has discussed the coming of the Son of Man and has hinted at the what will happen. Jesus wants the disciples to prepare for His passion and ultimately for salvation and heaven.

Summary: Jesus tells a parable of wise and foolish virgins. Ten virgins are waiting with their lamps for the bridegroom to arrive. Five of the wise virgins brought extra oil for their lamps, and the five foolish ones did not. They fell asleep waiting, and then at midnight the bridegroom arrived. The foolish virgins asked the wise ones for oil because they were running out and their lamps were failing. The wise ones said no because there was not enough for all of them. Then the foolish virgins went away to buy more, and when they returned the doors were locked, and they were not able to enter the wedding feast. Jesus warns his disciples, "Therefore, stay awake, for you know neither the day nor the hour."

Help students reflect: What do you do to prepare yourself for Christ in the Eucharist? What is one thing that you can do to prepare yourself for the Kingdom of Heaven? We cannot predict the time of our death, or the time of Jesus's return, so we should be ready at **any** moment and **every** moment.

ORDINARY TIME

Teacher Notes: Gospel Doodle Reflections Cycle Year "A"

The Parable of the Talents

The Thirty-Third Sunday of Ordinary Time
Matthew 25:14-30

Background information:
- A talent was a coin of high value. Only later in the Middle Ages did it come to be synonymous with money. By the 1500s talent would come to mean a special natural ability or gift.
- This parable is the second to last Jesus gives in Matthew before He begins His Passion, death, and resurrection.

Summary: Jesus tells a parable to explain who the Kingdom of God is for. Although His words may sound harsh at first, Jesus gives us this parable of common sense in words that are clear as can be. Those who are responsible in small matters will deserve to be entrusted with large matters. Those who are lazy or afraid will be entrusted with nothing. Our enjoyment of the Kingdom of God, in part, depends on the exercise of our talents.

Help students reflect: Take a moment to recognize the truth of Jesus's words. The one who practices more often makes the team. Take a moment to identify two or three of the talents God has given you. What are you doing to spend them for others? What do you do to develop your talents?

Our Lord Jesus Christ, King of the Universe

The Final Sunday of Ordinary Time
Matthew 25:31-46

Background information:
- This Gospel is the conclusion of Jesus's teaching prior to his Passion. In just 14 verses, Judas will go to the chief priests to betray Jesus.
- One interpretation of this Gospel is that "all the nations" means 'humanity' and "least ones" means 'those who are suffering'.
- Another interpretation is that "all the nations" means those 'people who have not accepted the Gospel'. "Least ones" means 'Christians who have suffered in order to attempt to spread the Gospel everywhere'.
- This Gospel contains the Corporal Works of Mercy: feed the hungry, welcome the stranger, clothe the naked, care for the sick, visit the imprisoned.

Summary: Jesus wraps up His teachings by telling us in matter-of-fact terms who is going to enjoy heaven and who is not. The Son of Man (Jesus) will come in judgement to separate the sheep and the goats. The sheep are the ones who cared for the least ones while the goats did not.

Help students reflect: Is it cruel for Jesus to judge humanity? Does there have to be a reward or a punishment for the way we live our lives here on earth? What are ways you can perform the Corporal Works of Mercy at this point in your life? How are we serving God when we do these things?

ORDINARY TIME

LENT

Teacher Notes: Gospel Doodle Reflections   **Cycle Year "A"**

Your Father Who Sees You

Ash Wednesday
Matthew 6:1-6, 16-18

Background information:
- Lent is a Latin word that means "springtime." Lent is all about new growth!
- The ashes used on Ash Wednesday come from the burning of the palm branches from the previous year's Palm Sunday.
- Did you know that a lot of current diets recommend "intermittent fasting" where only one meal is eaten a couple days every week?
- When Jesus talks about "hypocrites," He's referring to the Pharisees.

Summary: Here, Jesus teaches us to fast, give alms, and pray as a three-fold path to Christian holiness. He also teaches us to do all of these three in a spirit of humility, not to serve ourselves with attention. Finally, He reminds us that our Father always gives us His attention and is proud of the good things we do.

Help students reflect: If you have not done so, think of your goals for Lent. Prayer: How much time can you give to God? 1 Our Father every day? 1 Rosary a week? Talking to Him every day after school? Almsgiving: How much can you give to others? What is one game you could give to charity? Fasting: Try making your fasting about someone else! Do an extra chore at home, don't complain about whatever is served for dinner, etc.

Get Away, Satan!

The First Sunday of Lent
Matthew 4:1-11

Background information:
- Jesus goes into the desert before He starts any of His ministry of proclaiming the Kingdom of God, healing the sick, or forgiving sinners.
- "Forty days and nights" that Jesus spent in the desert are an allusion to the forty years Israelites spent in the desert after they had escaped Egypt. Although Israel was unfaithful and turned against God (remember the golden calf debacle?), Jesus remains faithful to God despite Satan's best efforts.

Summary: Jesus goes to the desert (for forty days!) to prepare for his ministry and Satan meets Jesus there to tempt him. Jesus defends himself from the temptations not with His divine power, but with the power of the truth of scripture and his own faithfulness.

Help students reflect:
Fasting, prayer, and almsgiving are difficult things to do and when we start trying to do these three we are bound to hear voices of discouragement. Don't listen to those voices! Also, since fasting, prayer, and almsgiving are all things God loves they are three things Satan hates. Try combating Satan's temptations by confidently reading the Bible. Finally, don't be afraid to tell Satan to go away. You have Jesus on your side and Satan is absolutely no match for that!

Teacher Notes: Gospel Doodle Reflections Cycle Year "A"

The Transfiguration

The Second Sunday of Lent
Matthew 17:1-9

Background information:
- This experience was given to James, John, and Peter to strengthen their faith before Jesus's Passion. In Matthew's gospel, we are only a little bit away from Palm Sunday here.
- Tents: The tents Peter references belong to a specific Jewish feast day recalling the Israelites' nomadic journey to the promised land.

Summary: Jesus takes James, John, and Peter up a mountain (near Jerusalem) to show them His glory. He does this to strengthen their faith. The disciples see Elijah and Moses speaking with Jesus and are astounded. Then they hear the voice of God and John, James, and Peter are thrown to the ground in fear.

Help students reflect: What would it mean to you to see the full glory of God? Can you remember a time when you have seen a little glimmer of God's glory? Does the disciples' fear make sense to you? Why? In the Transfiguration, Jesus gave his disciples something to remember during the tough times. What kinds of things do you remember to get you through difficult times?

The Woman at the Well

The Third Sunday of Lent
John 4:5-42

Background information:
- Samaritans and Jews were like staunch Democrats and Republicans; they did not get along.
- All the other women would have come to the well during the first rays of dawn when the temperature was much cooler. This woman comes at noon in the heat of the day because she is outcast from the other women.
- Living water means the freedom Jesus brings.
- Worshipping the Father in the Spirit and truth means Temple sacrifice is no longer necessary. To worship, it is only necessary to receive the Holy Spirit.

Summary: This is one of the most fantastic stories in the New Testament. Jesus meets a woman, outcast from her own community, who is a Samaritan: an enemy of Jews like Jesus. Jesus knows her shame, but offers her the merciful love of God. She is so shocked that she runs from the well and announces to all the Messiah. The community, who knew her as an outcast, is convicted by her freedom and comes to meet Jesus. Meanwhile, the disciples who have taken in Jesus's freedom like the Samaritan woman did are confused how Jesus could be neither hungry nor thirsty.

Help students reflect:
Have you ever had an experience where your shame was taken away and you were set free? Why would being set free from our shame be an important part of Lent? Does it make sense that true worship of God does not belong only to a special building?

The Woman at the Well
"Could He possibly be the Messiah?!"

We learn here that we can "worship the Father in Spirit and Truth," even when we are outside of Jerusalem, outside the temple, outside the church, etc. Draw your two favorite places to worship God other than a church.

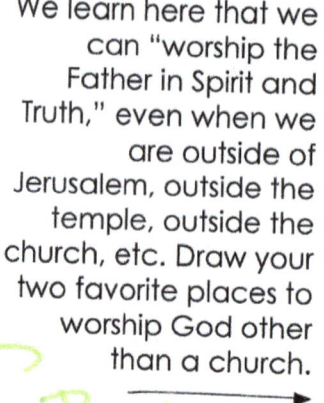

INVITING someone to CHURCH • *REMINDING a friend about Jesus* • *PLAYING worship music in the car*

Spread the Word

Word of Jesus begins to spread. The woman runs to tell the others that she has met the Messiah. No one else could have known all her sins. Reflect on a few different ways you have seen people spread the news about Jesus today. Write them above the arrows.

In each brick of the well, write a word that describes the woman. Inside the jug, write or sketch what Jesus means by "living water."

John 4:5-42

the woman:
SINNER • OUTCAST • SHAME • ISOLATED • UNWELCOME • SAD • ALONE • SURPRISED • AWED • BELIEVER • EMBARRASSED

Living Water: Freedom, Jesus, eternal life, Holy Spirit

© 2022 Catechetical Chameleon

Teacher Notes: Gospel Doodle Reflections Cycle Year "A"

The Man Born Blind

The Fourth Sunday of Lent
John 9:1-41

Background information:
- Using spit, making clay, and healing others are all prohibited by the Jewish on the Sabbath (day of rest) each week.
- Since Jesus is the Light of the World, he can bring light to blind eyes.
- The Pharisees show their spiritual blindness in refusing to see the Light of the World
- Physical infirmities were explained by reference to sin, either personal or familial.

Summary: Jesus encounters a blind man and heals him on the Sabbath. The Pharisees are outraged because Jesus's religion is so effective even apart from important Jewish rules, like Sabbath regulations (Pharisees never healed a blind man). So, the Pharisees become divided, and some threaten to cast the healed man and his parents from the synagogue. The man who was healed testifies to the truth of what Jesus did and shows the Pharisees a mirror to their blindness. Jesus convicts the Pharisees of the sin the healed man showed them.

Help students reflect: Are there people that we look down upon because of awkwardness, poverty, physical issues, or lack of talent? If we want to see the Light of the World we have to start looking with Jesus eyes. Then, we have to accept that Jesus is the Light of the World. So, the challenge this week is to stop judging others, but look for ways to build them up (even if it looks weird). Then, give thanks to Jesus for helping you to see the world this way.

The Raising of Lazarus

The Fifth Sunday of Lent
John 11:1-45

Background information:
- Lazarus is the brother of Mary and Martha. Mary is the one who anointed Jesus and washed his feet with her hair. It's not clear if they are the same Mary and Martha from Luke 10:38-42.
- This event convinces the Sanhedrin that they must kill Jesus.
- It was dangerous for Jesus to return to Lazarus, because the Jews had just recently tried to stone him (to death) there (John 10:31).
- Catholics believe Jesus was thoroughly human. So, of course, he wept when he saw the funeral crowd for one of his friends.

Summary: Jesus's friend Lazarus dies and Jesus waits three days to go to him. Jesus waits so that more people may be more convinced that Jesus is "the resurrection and the life." Jesus, though he has the power to raise Lazarus, weeps for the death of his friend. Finally, Jesus shows us that everything is possible through Him so long as we have faith.

Help students reflect: Do you think that Jesus has ever wept for you? What sorts of things does Jesus weep for today? Do you think Jesus knew how dangerous it would be for Him to perform this miracle? What are some things in your own life that you could ask Jesus to give new life to? What holds you back from having faith that Jesus can raise up these situations?

The Man Born Blind
John 9:1-41

The actions Jesus took to heal the man's sight were not allowed on the Sabbath according to Jewish law.

Speech bubbles:
- "This is good. Let them stay."
- "It's a MIRACLE!"
- "Surely this man is from God!"

Side A / **Side B** — **PHARISEES**

Why did the Pharisees disagree? What were they split about? Write some example statements that people nearby may have heard from each side as they debated.

Speech bubbles:
- "This was SINFUL"
- "The laws say not to do such things on the Sabbath."
- "It's not right. Send them away."

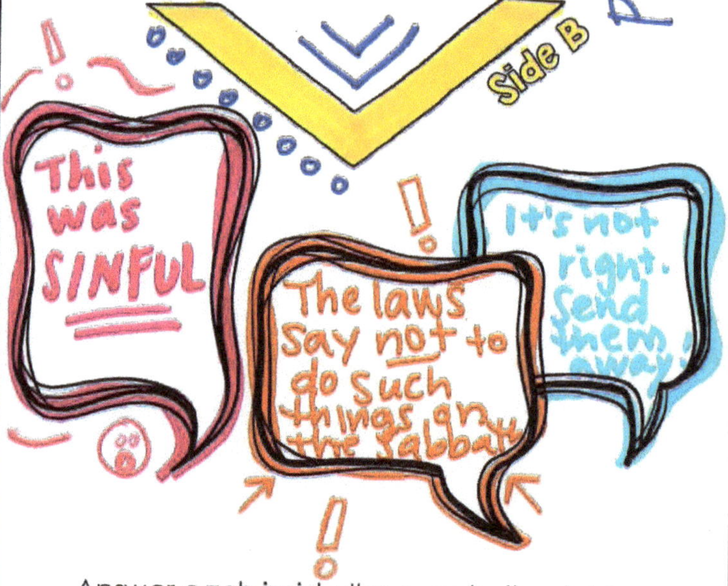

Answer each inside the eyes to the right:
1. In what way was the man blind?
2. In what way were the Pharisees blind?
3. In what way(s) are **you** ever blind?
4. In what way(s) are people of today's world sometimes blind?

Lord, open my eyes...

SIGHT

1. literally + physically BLIND — bodily eyes — the man
2. figuratively BLIND TO THE TRUTH of the MIRACLE — the Pharisees
3. to God, to the needs of people around me, working in my life — me
4. unwilling BLIND TO GOD'S TRUTH!! to really see — people today: different ways to be BLIND

Teacher Notes: Gospel Doodle Reflections Cycle Year "A"

The Entrance into Jerusalem

LENT

Palm Sunday
Matthew 26:14-27:66

Background information:
- By the time Jesus enters Jerusalem (especially after raising Lazarus), most people are convinced that He is the Messiah. Most of them, however, have always imagined that the Messiah will be a kind of divine soldier who will free Israel from Roman occupation and oppression: not exactly what Jesus had in mind.
- Jesus, the Messiah, enters Jerusalem before Passover, a time when tens of thousands of Jews would journey into the city to celebrate the Israelites' freedom from Egyptian oppression. Imagine USA being run by England again. And now this guy we all think is the Messiah travels to Washington DC for the Fourth of July. England would certainly be on edge. That's how Pontius Pilate felt.
- Crucifixion was the worst possible humiliation and torture used by the Roman Empire to subjugate political dissidents. It remains one of the worst tortures in human history.

Summary: Jesus enters Jerusalem to celebrate Passover with His disciples. Judas seizes the opportunity to betray Jesus. Jesus, recognizing what is about to happen, goes to the garden to pray. It is Jesus's last opportunity to flee without showing His power. Jesus is arrested, put on a mock trial overnight, and condemned by morning on trumped up charges. He is scourged, crowned with thorns, beaten and abused. He never lashes out, but actually seeks to comfort those He encounters, including His own mother. Ultimately, He carries his cross to Golgotha just outside the city, where He is crucified and dies. He is almost completely abandoned and betrayed by His disciples, His closest friends. Only His mother, Mary, and a man named Joseph accompany Him. Joseph receives His body and prepares it for burial. Jesus is locked in a tomb.

Help students reflect: Welcome to Holy Week. Why was it so easy for people to celebrate Jesus's entrance into Jerusalem with palms and songs and then crucify Him only five days later? How did Jesus know that He was going to be betrayed? Do you think Jesus ever stopped loving Judas?

If Jesus was God, why did He allow Himself to suffer so much?

You absolutely have to set aside time this week to be with Jesus. Let the Gospel account of His Passion convict you of His love for you.

Teacher Notes: Gospel Doodle Reflections   **Cycle Year "A"**

The Last Supper

Holy Thursday
John 13:1-15

Background information:
- On Holy Thursday, Jesus celebrated a Passover meal with His disciples. This meal is the most important ceremony in the Jewish religion which remembers how God rescued them from slavery in Egypt and brought them to the Land of Promise.
- When Jesus celebrates this meal the night before He dies, He is trying to show how God will again rescue His people from their slavery to sin and selfishness. This saving event is His death on Good Friday.
- Feet got very dirty back then from walking on dusty dirt roads in sandals all day.
- The act of washing another's feet, in Jesus's day, was one that could not be required of the lowliest Jewish slave. It is an allusion to the humiliating death of the crucifixion.

Summary: Jesus hosts the Passover meal with the disciples. At this meal He performs the task of a slave by washing His disciples' feet. The disciples protest, but Jesus admonishes them: if you do not let me serve you, you will never receive my salvation.

Help students reflect: Why did Jesus choose to suffer and die this way for all of us? Why did He choose to allow Himself (remember that He is the almighty God) to be humiliated by performing the worst chore/labor in washing His disciples' feet? Why does He ask us to wash one another's feet? Is selfishness the thing we most need to be saved from?

The Death of Jesus Christ

Good Friday
John 18:1-19:42

Background information:
- Peter was Jesus's best friend when he denied that he even knew Jesus.
- Crucifixion was public murder: a state-sponsored terrorism reserved for men and women who acted against the Roman Empire.
- Philosophers and theologians have interpreted Jesus's line, "It is finished," not only as the end of Jesus's life but as the "finishing" or "completion" of human history.

Summary: Jesus is betrayed by Judas and taken away by the Jewish temple guards. Jesus is tried by the Jewish authorities in a mock trial and convicted while He is abandoned by most of his disciples. The Jews take Jesus to Pilate, the local Roman governor, because only Romans had authority to crucify. Pilate finds Jesus innocent, but obeys the pressure of the mob, has Jesus scourged, and hands Jesus over for crucifixion. Jesus dies nailed to a cross and is buried.

Help students reflect: What did Jesus do to deserve so much betrayal, abandonment, abuse, lies, torture, humiliation, and embarrassment? Everyone in the story (except Pontius Pilate and Jesus's own mother) wanted to blame Jesus (for what?) and destroy Him. Why? Why did they want this? What did He do to deserve such universal condemnation? Why did everyone feel so victimized by Jesus? Were their feelings justified? Were their feelings true? Do we ever blame innocent people? Do we ever allow ourselves to be angry at people who are just and true?

Teacher Notes: Gospel Doodle Reflections — Cycle Year "A"

The Empty Tomb

Easter Sunday
John 20:1-9

Background information:
• The crucifixion and the empty tomb are two of the best documented events in human history.
• The resurrection is the most influential event in documented human history.
• The tomb was guarded by Roman soldiers, but John found it empty. The arrangement of the burial cloths in the tomb made John believe that it had not been robbed, and that Jesus had risen from the dead as He had promised.

Summary: On Sunday, Mary of Magdala (and perhaps some other women) went to the tomb in grief, but Mary was stunned to find the tomb open and empty. She ran to the disciples and found Simon Peter and John, who then ran to see for themselves what had happened. The disciples found the tomb empty and slowly began to believe that Jesus had risen.

Help students reflect: Jesus defeated death, and He did it in such a way that to His followers, it was not about Himself at all, but about strengthening all of their faith in God. Where in your life do you need to see a resurrection? In your circumstances? In yourself? Can you pray to God that the things that are weighing you down will be made light? Can you pray to God that He would give you the grace of believing in Him?

Peace Be With You

Divine Mercy Sunday
John 20:19-31

Background information:
• This may be the same resurrection appearance as the famous story of "Doubting Thomas."
• Resurrected Jesus still appears in human form but is able to enter into locked rooms.
• The breathing calls to mind the breath of life God breathed into Adam in Genesis. Now Jesus gives new life to the disciples who had been "dead" because of grief and despair.

Summary: After Jesus's death by mob violence His disciples had to hide themselves from the rest of the Jewish community which was seeking to root out any remnants of Jesus. In a locked room, they gathered in secret for several days, until finally Jesus appeared to them in person, at once. Jesus gave them peace and showed them His scars. The disciples were able to rejoice again and received the Holy Spirit. Together with the Holy Spirit, Jesus gave them the authority to forgive sins.

Help students reflect: Peace is the fruit of a Christian life because we have the knowledge of the resurrection and because we make decisions that keep our life peaceful and in harmony. Take a moment to reflect on how peaceful your life is. What could be improved? Jesus gave the disciples authority to forgive sins. Today that authority remains with our bishops and is passed to us through our priests. What does confession mean to you?

Teacher Notes: Gospel Doodle Reflections   **Cycle Year "A"**

The Road to Emmaus

EASTER

Third Sunday of Easter
Luke 24:13-35

Background information:
• The disciples in this story did not believe in the Resurrection, although they had heard of the empty tomb. That is why they are walking away from Jerusalem.
• "It was necessary that the Messiah had to suffer" means that the Messiah, of course, would have to suffer, given that the world is the way that it is. Jesus did not absolutely have to suffer, but because the world is the way that it is, He suffered.

Summary: Two disciples, dejected and depressed by the death of Jesus, leave the Christian community in Jerusalem and go off (probably to their former way of life) to Emmaus. On their journey, they encounter a stranger who asks them what they are talking about. They recount the story of Jesus's crucifixion as well as their broken-heartedness about the death of the Messiah. Jesus corrects them and then breaks bread with them. At this, the disciples realize the stranger is Jesus and return to Jerusalem to tell the community what happened to them.

Help students reflect: Are we tempted to walk away sometimes? What kind of situations are we tempted to walk away from? Have we ever been turned around and sent back to what we were tempted to walk away from? Jesus wants us to recommit to love: return to loving the people we are called to love in life. You can do it!

I Am the Gate

Fourth Sunday of Easter
John 10:1-10

Background information:
• This Sunday is called Good Shepherd Sunday because in all three cycles (Year A, B, and C) this Sunday's Gospel reading has to do with Jesus the Good Shepherd.
• This Gospel falls in between the stories of the Healing of the Man Born Blind and the Raising of Lazarus: both stories detail the conflict between Jesus's good works and the Pharisees anger at the power of Jesus.

Summary: After healing and before raising Lazarus, Jesus teaches us that He is the true teacher: the one who will protect us and lead us to green pastures. He teaches this in order to contrast Himself to the Pharisees (who are the thieves and robbers) so that people will know the difference between Jesus's religion which really loves people and the religion of the Pharisees which has become too caught up in worldly regulations and practices and is forgetting to love people.

Help students reflect: Who has been a good shepherd in your life (someone that has helped you to focus on really taking care of people)? Who leads you to green pastures? Who protects you? How can you be a Good Shepherd for others?

Teacher Notes: Gospel Doodle Reflections　　　　　　　　　　　　　　　　**Cycle Year "A"**

The Way, Truth, and Life

Fifth Sunday of Easter
John 14:1-12

Background information:
• Jesus is God and He is also the Father's (who is also God) bridge to the created world.
• This Gospel is an exhortation to faith: Jesus trying to convince us that we really do need to believe in Him if we want to live together with God.
• Knowing the Truth means having a relationship with Jesus who is the Truth. Knowing the Way means understanding His guidance for how to live. Having the Life means having a relationship with Jesus who gives us real Life.

Summary: During the Last Supper, just before Jesus was set to die, He teaches His disciples for a long time and tells them that they must believe in Him. Jesus knew how hard it was going to be for His disciples to keep their faith once He died, so He starts now trying to impress on them the seriousness of who He is: He is God, and He is the Way, the Truth and the Life. He is the only path to the Father.

Help students reflect: Faith isn't easy: it is the biggest commitment we'll ever make. Like committing to good grades, success in sports, or being a good son/daughter, faith means committing every day to doing the right things that will help us reach our goals. Have you chosen to make your goal living in Heaven with the Father? How strong is your faith commitment?

The Spirit of Truth

Sixth Sunday of Easter
John 14:15-21

Background information:
• The Spirit is the animating, energizing part of human life. Jesus says that the Truth also has an animating, energizing part: the Holy Spirit (the Advocate).
• An "Advocate" can be a legal defense attorney, or is a spokesman, mediator, intercessor, comforter, and consoler. The Advocate is a direct contrast to "The Satan" which is the legal *accuser* of the world. The Advocate is on OUR side and will defend us and have our back.
• The Holy Spirit teaches, witnesses to Jesus, judges the world, and is the continuous presence on earth of Jesus who returned to the Father. The Holy Spirit is God and the reason for our unity and community: we are together in the Holy Spirit.

Summary: Again, as a part of His Last Supper teachings, just before Jesus goes to die, He teaches the disciples about the third person of the Trinity: The Advocate. The Advocate is the presence of Jesus on earth and will never leave us alone, orphaned, or without the ability to love Jesus and follow His commands. With The Advocate we are capable of true love.

Help students reflect: Do you ever think about God as a Trinity? How do you relate to the Father? How about to the Son? Do you connect with the Holy Spirit? Do you connect with the language of "The Advocate?" Have you ever felt like the Holy Spirit was an advocate for you? Do you see Jesus when you love people really well? How can we get better at seeing Jesus?

Teacher Notes: Gospel Doodle Reflections　　　　　　　　　　　　**Cycle Year "A"**

The Hour Has Come

EASTER

Seventh Sunday of Easter
John 17:1-11

Background information:
• This prayer is Jesus's last extended word to His disciples before He is arrested in the garden.
• Throughout the Gospel of John, Jesus emphasizes the union that exists between Him and the Father.
• Verse 3 is the only time in any Gospel that Jesus refers to Himself as the "Christ."

Summary: At the end of the Last Supper, Jesus offers a long prayer that includes these lines: He explains that His hour to be glorified by the Father has come, that He has revealed the Father to His disciples, and that He has separated His disciples from simply being in the world in order to belong in a more exclusive way to the Father.

Help students reflect: When will your hour come? Maybe it will come at exam time, or when you have to make a tough choice about friends. Maybe your hour will come when your brother or a parent asks you for help. Whatever it is, your hour will be a time to either flop or to be glorified by the Father. If you want the Father to glorify you when your hour comes, you must start glorifying Him now. In other words, Jesus is telling us: if you want Godly success, you must worship God. How successful are you? How prepared are you for your hour? Do you worship God?

Go Make Disciples of All Nations

Ascension of Our Lord
Matthew 28:16-20

Background information:
• In the Bible, many major events happen on top of mountains.
• This Gospel contains one of the most explicit expressions of New Testament belief in the Trinity; it is the same formula we use today for Baptisms, two *thousand* years later!
• Depending on your diocese, Ascension is celebrated on a Thursday or Sunday.

Summary: The resurrected Jesus tells His disciples to meet Him at a mountain top. There, He appears to them and they worship but tentatively, so that He can tell they don't totally believe in Him. He reminds them of His universal power and gives them a universal mission: to make disciples of all nations. And He tells them that He will be with them always.

Help students reflect: This event happens before Pentecost. This means that after the disciples worship Jesus and doubt, after He tells them again about His universal power, and even after Jesus gives them a universal mission, the disciples still go back and hide together in a room in Jerusalem. Jesus loved the disciples right where they were at, but yet too much to leave them there. Jesus loves you right where you are, but yet too much to leave you there. He gives us missions we are not ready for, but will always send His Holy Spirit to empower us to complete the mission. What mission has Jesus asked you to perform? Where do you see that in your own life? Where do you need encouragement? Where do you pray the Holy Spirit is coming to help you?

Teacher Notes: Gospel Doodle Reflections — Cycle Year "A"

Peace Be With You

Pentecost
John 20:19-23

Background information:
- Jesus breathes on His disciples and reminds us how God first breathed life into Adam in Genesis: the Holy Spirit gives us Life.
- Jesus breathes the Holy Spirit onto His disciples and tells them to be at peace and to forgive: the Holy Spirit gives us unity with each other.
- The power to forgive sins happens most of all in the Sacrament of Reconciliation (according to the Council of Trent).

Summary: The disciples were hiding in the upper room and, on a Sunday, Jesus appeared there and showered peace and the Holy Spirit onto His disciples. Jesus showed the disciples His wounds in order to strengthen their faith and they rejoiced and believed. Finally, Jesus gives them the power to forgive sins.

Help students reflect: Take a deep breath. Being Christian is not easy, but living in fear is never an option. Sometimes in life we have to take a deep breath before we can move forward in faith, hope, love, and the joy of knowing God. Have you ever experienced this? Can you share a time when you were nervous, but were able to turn fear into confidence and step forward? How can you prepare now for the next time you'll need to step out of fear?

One way to prepare is to practice meditative prayer. Meditative prayer, according to the Catechism, is a way of understanding God's revelation and the purpose of the Christian life in order to respond to what the Lord is asking of us (CCC, 2705). To start, find a quiet place where you can sit or lie down for at least five minutes. Then, take a few deep breaths and ask the Holy Spirit to be with you. Then, ask the Holy Spirit what message He wants to give you today. Take a few more deep breaths and sit and listen deeply. After some minutes, ask the Holy Spirit how He wants you to take that message out into the world. Take a few more deep breaths and listen again. When you are done, thank the Father and the Son and the Holy Spirit, and then write down what you heard.

EASTER

Teacher Notes: Gospel Doodle Reflections　　　　　　　　　　　　　　Cycle Year "A"

Immaculate Conception

Feast of the Immaculate Conception of Mary
Luke 1:26-38

Background information: Some people mistakenly think that the Immaculate Conception is about Jesus being conceived, but it is actually about Mary being conceived without sin from the very beginning of her life.

Summary: Mary is "full of grace" to the point that she is completely without sin. She is pure and free of the stain and corruption that other humans are susceptible to because of original sin. Her special sanctifying grace was present from before her own birth, as she was blessed by God in advance. She would bear Jesus, and therefore God's grace made her holy and pure.

Help students reflect: What does this show about God's plan for Jesus, that He made Mary immaculate from her conception and through her entire life? How can I strive to be more like Mary, despite my own imperfection? How would I answer such a large request or challenge from God if an angel came to me? How would my own response compare to Mary's reply of "may it be done to me according to your word."?

Mary, Mother of God

Solemnity of Mary, Holy Mother of God
Luke 2:16-21

Background information: Mary had followed through with God's plan, and we celebrate her as the Mother of God. We have many titles for Mary because she is so special.

Summary: Jesus is finally born, a God coming to earth through human birth, made possible through Mary. This incredible event did not go unnoticed by the shepherds, and would later come to be known throughout the entire world. Mary is the human mother to a newborn baby who is both God and man. As the Mother of God, we honor her.

Help students reflect: Mary "kept all these things, reflecting on them in her heart." Put yourself in Mary's position for a moment in your imagination. How do you think it felt for the shepherds to come visit her newborn, after knowing what the angel had told her. Now think ahead to Jesus's adult life. We know His future, and the suffering Mary would have to endure later on in His story. She was central to something incredibly special, that caused the shepherds to glorify God. Jesus was such a gift! Think about Mary's part in all of this and what her reflections in her heart may have been.

Teacher Notes: Gospel Doodle Reflections Cycle Year "A"

Feast of the Assumption
Luke 1:39-56

Background information:
- Sometimes, Mary is compared to the Ark of the Covenant, because she carried / held God's word (come to life!)
- Pope Pius XII declared Mary's Assumption into Heaven as part of our official "dogma" for Catholics in 1950.
- There is a difference between the word used for Jesus **ascending** into heaven, and Mary being **assumed** into heaven, because Jesus rose up out of his own power while Mary was assumed out of God's power, not her own.

Summary: This feast day is about Mary being assumed into heaven, body and soul. She was without sin and was pure. To honor her, God carried her right up to heaven without her having to die in the same way that we do. She is now considered "Queen of Heaven."

Help students reflect: Think how challenging Mary's life on earth was. She had to watch her son suffer and die in a horrible way. Can you see why Jesus saved her from having to go through the same bodily death that we all must endure? What an honor, to be the only human to ever enter the kingdom of Heaven without her body having to go through the usual earthly decay. Her body was sacred to God and she is still very much respected by all of us today.

All Saints Day
Matthew 5:1-12a

Background information:
- Saints (with a capital "S") are canonized, official saints. When we use a lowercase "s" for the word saints, it represents all of the people in heaven. All of the good people of God who have died and gone to heaven are part of the communion of saints.
- All Souls Day is different from All Saints Day because it also includes the faithful people who have died that are not yet in heaven (like those in purgatory). They may be repentant, but have not yet fully entered into the glory of heaven.
- This holy day was originally started to honor martyrs (those who died for their faith).

Summary: This feast day is for celebrating all of the saints, both known and unknown. They are often also referred to as the "faithful departed," because they have died and are in the kingdom of heaven.

Help students reflect: This is a good day to learn about a Saint or choose a favorite Saint. You might be surprised how much you have in common with some of the canonized Saints if you do a little research. Say a prayer that you will someday become a saint in heaven yourself.

BONUS PAGES

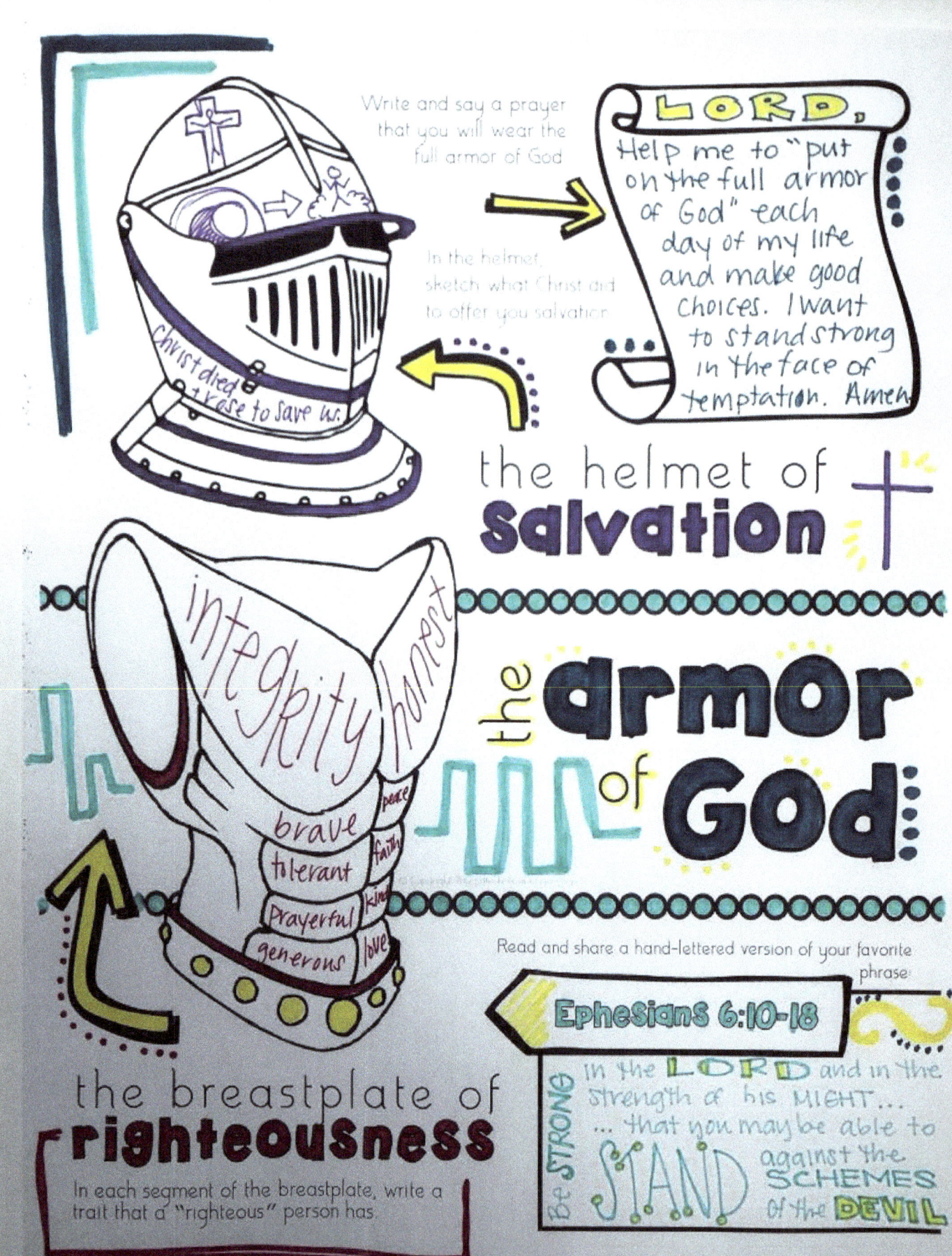

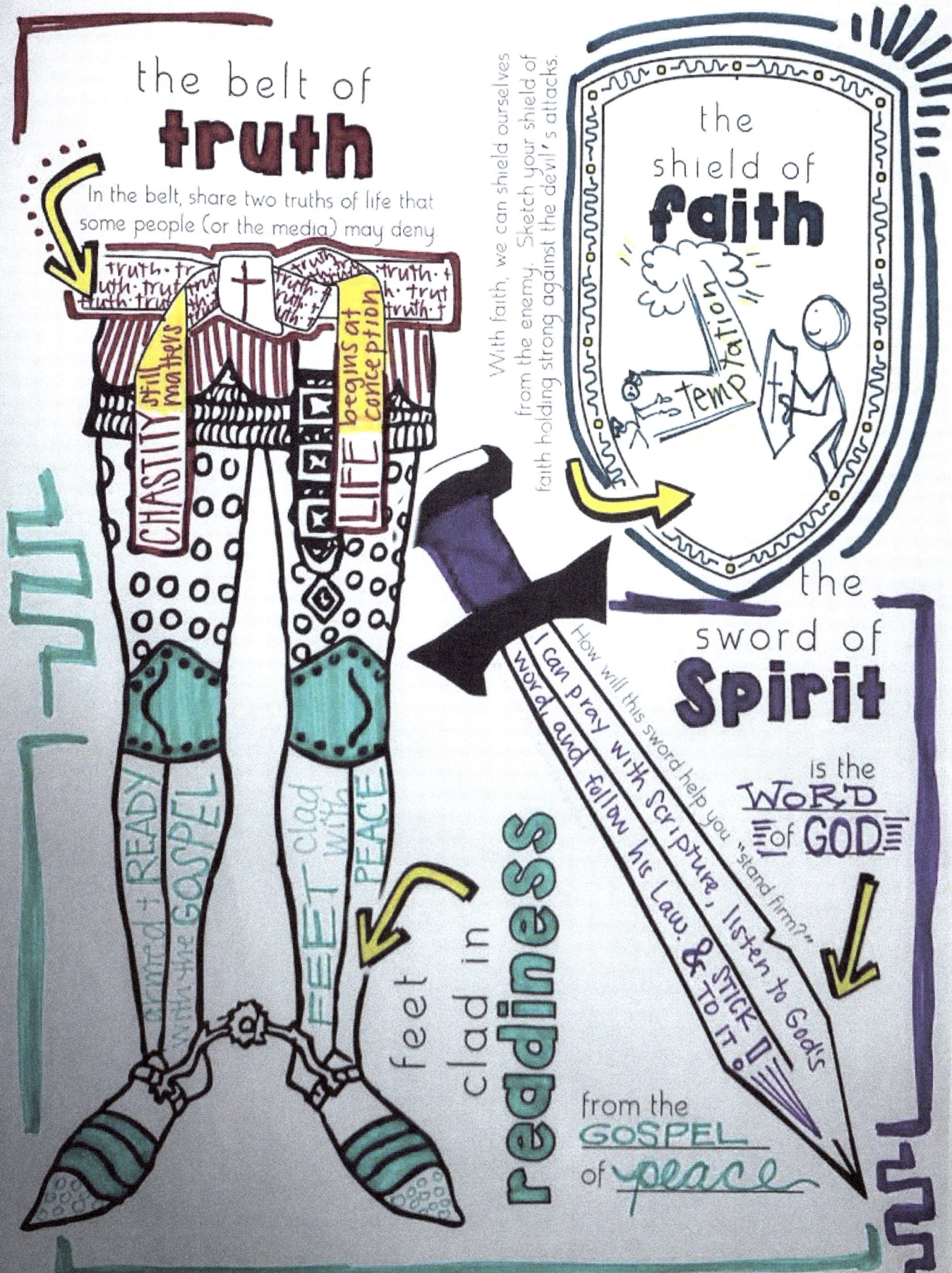

- Color the words around the perimeter of the calendar using the color listed.
- Fill in the blanks to show what each color represents.
- Write the season of the church year inside each sector.
- Show the seasons of the regular calendar year outside of the circle.

Name: Answer Key / Teacher Guide

The Liturgical Calendar

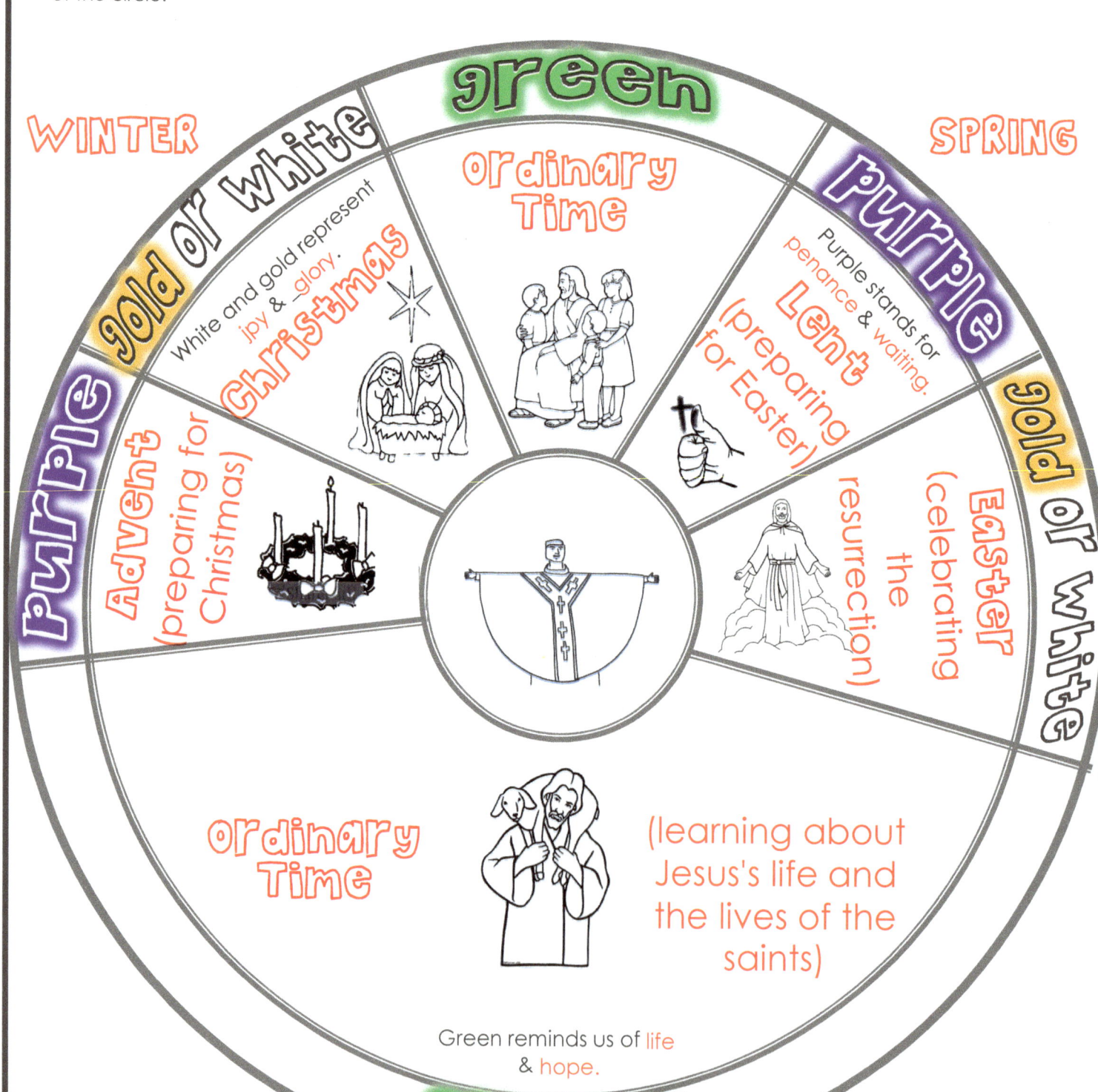

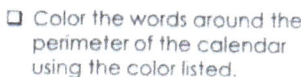

The Liturgical Calendar

- ☐ Color the words around the perimeter of the calendar using the color listed.
- ☐ Fill in the blanks to show what each color represents
- ☐ Write the season of the church year inside each sector
- ☐ Show the season of the regular calendar year outside of the circle.

Name: _____

WINTER

SPRING

green — ORDINARY TIME

gold or white — White and gold represent JOY & GLORY — CHRISTMAS

purple — ADVENT — preparing for Christmas...

purple — Purple stands for PRAYING & WAITING — LENT — preparing for Easter

gold or white — EASTER

green — ORDINARY TIME — We learn about the life of Jesus... and about the lives of the saints. Green reminds us of LIFE & HOPE.

The Colors of the priest's vestments match the color of the liturgical season.

FALL

SUMMER

© Copyright 2016 Catechetical Chameleon

www.ingramcontent.com/pod-product-compliance
Lightning Source LLC
Chambersburg PA
CBHW061119070526
44583CB00028B/3339